Art-Based Social Enterprise, Young Creatives and the Forces of Marginalisation

Grace McQuilten · Amy Spiers ·
Kim Humphery · Peter Kelly

Art-Based Social Enterprise, Young Creatives and the Forces of Marginalisation

palgrave
macmillan

Grace McQuilten
School of Art
RMIT University
Melbourne, VIC, Australia

Amy Spiers
School of Art
RMIT University
Melbourne, VIC, Australia

Kim Humphery
School of Global, Urban & Social Studies
RMIT University
Melbourne, VIC, Australia

Peter Kelly
School of Education
Deakin University
Bundoora, VIC, Australia

ISBN 978-3-031-10924-9   ISBN 978-3-031-10925-6 (eBook)
https://doi.org/10.1007/978-3-031-10925-6

© The Author(s), under exclusive license to Springer Nature Switzerland AG 2022
This work is subject to copyright. All rights are solely and exclusively licensed by the Publisher, whether the whole or part of the material is concerned, specifically the rights of translation, reprinting, reuse of illustrations, recitation, broadcasting, reproduction on microfilms or in any other physical way, and transmission or information storage and retrieval, electronic adaptation, computer software, or by similar or dissimilar methodology now known or hereafter developed.
The use of general descriptive names, registered names, trademarks, service marks, etc. in this publication does not imply, even in the absence of a specific statement, that such names are exempt from the relevant protective laws and regulations and therefore free for general use.
The publisher, the authors, and the editors are safe to assume that the advice and information in this book are believed to be true and accurate at the date of publication. Neither the publisher nor the authors or the editors give a warranty, expressed or implied, with respect to the material contained herein or for any errors or omissions that may have been made. The publisher remains neutral with regard to jurisdictional claims in published maps and institutional affiliations.

Cover illustration: © John Rawsterne/patternhead.com

This Palgrave Macmillan imprint is published by the registered company Springer Nature Switzerland AG
The registered company address is: Gewerbestrasse 11, 6330 Cham, Switzerland

Acknowledgements

We would firstly like to acknowledge the significant intellectual contribution of Professor Deborah Warr, who as part of our research team always pushed us to look closer, to think more carefully, to attend to issues of equity and access at every corner, and perhaps most importantly, to keep going back to the voices of young creatives. Dr. Perri Campbell was a key member of our team from 2017 to 2018, and her insights on youth cultures and creativity were invaluable. We would also like to thank Chiara Grassia, our talented Ph.D. candidate whose work on understanding the role of 'safe spaces' in supporting young creatives to imagine their futures is making a great contribution to the fields of education and community arts development. We extend our appreciation to our generous colleagues across the Schools of Art, Education and Global & Urban Social Studies at RMIT University for their critical feedback, collegiality and support—with a special shout out to Dr. Ruth DeSouza for pointing us back towards Eve Tuck's humanising approach to research with young people. We would also like to take the opportunity to acknowledge the late Professor Andy Furlong (the University of Glasgow), who prior to his premature death in January 2017 had played an important role in developing some of the ideas that framed our original project proposal, and who was to be a Partner Investigator on the project. Andy's profile, track record and influence in sociologies of youth are profound. But, importantly, Andy's intellect, humour, collegiality and willingness to mentor and collaborate continue to be sorely missed.

Above all, we would like to acknowledge and thank the generous contributions of artists, staff and students across the twelve art-based social enterprises that we surveyed as part of our study, and in particular at our three case study organisations Youthworx, The Social Studio and Outer Urban Projects. At Youthworx, Jon Staley, Keith Waters, David Mackenzie and Nicola Innes provided enormous insights into the importance of providing engaging training for young creatives disengaged from mainstream schooling. At The Social Studio, our research was embraced by Dewi Cooke, Cate Coleman, Eugenia Flynn and Aleksandra Nedjelkovic, who expanded our thinking about the complexities, and possibilities, of the ASE model. And at Outer Urban Projects, Kate Gillick, David Ralph and Irene Vela welcomed us into the 'OUP family' and have inspired a range of critical approaches that have impacted on the findings in the book. We have immensely enjoyed collaborating with these colleagues and young creatives in co-producing exhibitions and events. We further acknowledge that author Grace McQuilten is co-founder and former CEO (2009–2014) of The Social Studio.

This book has emerged from a five-year, qualitative research project titled 'Art Based Social Enterprises and Marginalised Young People's Transitions', led by Professor Peter Kelly, Dr. Grace McQuilten, Associate Professor Kim Humphery and Professor Deb Warr, across two Australian Universities including RMIT University (Melbourne) and Charles Sturt University (Wagga). The research was supported fully by the Australian Government through the Australian Research Council's Discovery Projects funding scheme (project DP170100547). The views expressed herein are those of the authors and are not necessarily those of the Australian Government or Australian Research Council. Parts of Chapter 5, 'The Social Studio: Hope and Pragmatic Ambition', have been adapted from a previous journal article '"Art is different": Material practice, learning and co-making at The Social Studio', published in the *Journal of Arts and Communities* (10[2], pp. 19–33) by Intellect Publishers. Reproduced with permission of The Licensor through PLSclear.

Contents

1 Introduction: Artistic Practice and Social Outcomes in a Market-Driven Landscape   1
2 Precarious Youth and Digital Futures   27
3 The Youthworx Model: Disengaged Young People and Creative Digital Training   41
4 Fashioning a Future: Material Practice, Creativity and Sustainable Economies   65
5 The Social Studio: Hope and Pragmatic Ambition   81
6 Creative Practice, Cultural Citizenship and the Urban Fringe   107
7 Outer Urban Projects: Community Building Versus Mainstreaming   121
8 Conclusion   145

Index   157

About the Authors

Dr. Grace McQuilten is an art historian, curator and writer and Associate Professor in the School of Art at RMIT University. She was born and grew up on Dja Dja Warrung country and now lives and works on the lands of the Wurundjeri peoples of the Eastern Kulin nations. She completed her Ph.D. in art history at the University of Melbourne in 2008. She is the author of *Art as Enterprise: Social & Economic Engagement in Contemporary Art* (co-authored with Dr. Anthony White, IB Tauris, 2016) and *Art in Consumer Culture* (Ashgate Publishing, 2011) and has published widely on contemporary art and design. Alongside her academic career, she has worked extensively in social enterprise, community development, public art and curatorship, and is deeply committed to the relationship between artistic practice and social change.

Dr. Amy Spiers is an artist and researcher living on the unceded lands of the Kulin nation in so-called Melbourne, Australia. She completed a Master of Fine Art in 2011 and a Ph.D. in 2018 at the Victorian College of the Arts. She has presented socially-engaged art projects across Australia and internationally, including at Monash University Museum of Art (Melbourne), MONA FOMA festival (Hobart) and the 2015 Vienna Biennale. She has published academic and arts writing widely and most recently edited *Let's Go Outside: Art in Public* (co-edited with Charlotte Day and Callum Morton, Monash University Publishing, 2022). She is currently a Vice Chancellor Postdoctoral Research Fellow at RMIT School of Art, as well as co-editing a book with Genevieve Grieves on Indigenous settler relations in Australian contemporary art and memorial practices (Springer, forthcoming 2022).

Kim Humphery is Associate Professor in sociology and social theory at RMIT University and holds degrees from the universities of Melbourne and Cambridge in politics, social theory and history. She lives and works on the lands of the Wurundjeri peoples of the Kulin nations. Since the mid-1990s, she has developed a national profile for her socio-cultural work in Indigenous health and cross-cultural research ethics. She has also researched and written on community arts and wellbeing. Internationally, however, she is best known for her work in the history and sociology of consumption and has published extensively on ethical consumption and enterprise. Most recently, she has turned to researching theories of trans and gender diversity. Her major publications include: *Shelf Life: Supermarkets and The Changing Cultures of Consumption* (CUP 1998 & 2011) and *Excess: Anti-Consumerism in the West* (Polity 2010).

Peter Kelly is a Professor of Education in the School of Education at Deakin University. Peter's current research interests include a critical engagement with young people, their wellbeing, resilience and enterprise, and the challenges associated with the emergence of the Anthropocene. In the context of the COVID-19 pandemic, these interests are framing the development of a research agenda titled: COVID-19 and Young People's Well-being, Education, Training and Employment Pathways: Scenarios for Young People's Sustainable Futures. Peter's previous books include: Social Justice in Times of Crisis and Hope: Young People, Wellbeing and the Politics of Education, Re-thinking Young People's Marginalisation: Beyond Neo-Liberal Futures?, Young People and the

Politics of Outrage and Hope, A Critical Youth Studies for the 21st Century; The Self as Enterprise: Foucault and the Spirit of 21st Century Capitalism, and Working in Jamie's Kitchen: Salvation, Passion and Young Workers.

List of Figures

Fig. 1.1	A still from *Emerging* (2020), a video made by students of Youthworx, a media production social enterprise based in Melbourne (Image courtesy of the artists and Youthworx)	4
Fig. 1.2	Emerging fashion designer, Nancy Oziya, at work at The Social Studio, a fashion-based social enterprise in Melbourne (Photograph: Teva Cosic)	14
Fig. 1.3	A still from *Silence, Dance, Poetry* (2020), a video by Outer Urban Projects performing artist Damian Seddon (Image courtesy of the artist and Outer Urban Projects)	20
Fig. 3.1	Youthworx video installation, *Emerging* (2020), installed at Bus Projects, Collingwood (Photograph: Lucy Foster)	44
Fig. 3.2	Youthworx video installation, *Emerging* (2020), installed at Bus Projects, Collingwood (Photograph: Lucy Foster)	57
Fig. 3.3	A 'making-of' scene from *Emerging* (2020) (Image courtesy of the artists and Youthworx)	57
Fig. 5.1	Asia Hassan, *Take It Off!, 2019*. Asiyam Label (Image courtesy of Asiyam)	83

Fig. 5.2	Muhubo Sulieman leads a weaving workshop at The Social Studio in August 2019 (Photograph Teva Cosic)	92
Fig. 5.3	Muhubo Sulieman instructs one of the researchers and a student of The Social Studio how to do finger weaving in August 2019 (Photograph Teva Cosic)	93
Fig. 5.4	Twich Women's Sewing Collective founder Abuk Bol (far right) with co-founders (left to right) Nyachol John, Ayen Bol and Akech Majok (Image courtesy of Twich Women's Sewing Collective)	97
Fig. 7.1	A promotional image for Hume Studios (Image courtesy of Outer Urban Projects)	124
Fig. 7.2	Artist Ruci Kaisila performing at Hume Studios (Image courtesy of Outer Urban Projects)	132
Fig. 7.3	Image developed in the OUP's organisational mapping workshop facilitated by the research team, August 2018	141

1

Introduction: Artistic Practice and Social Outcomes in a Market-Driven Landscape

Abstract This chapter explores the context in which art-based social enterprises (ASEs) are engaging young creatives in education and training and supporting their pathways to the creative industries. In doing so, it also sets the terms for how this book aims to address the complex intersecting issues of marginality and entrepreneurship, particularly in relation to young creatives from socially, economically and culturally diverse backgrounds. This chapter examines several key issues, including (1) the *social turn* in contemporary art, in which artistic practices are engaged with the lives of people and communities and with a spirit of collectivism aimed at addressing a range of issues from social exclusion to climate change; (2) rapid growth in social enterprise models across a range of sectors, including the creative industries that has been spurred, in part, by increasing economic pragmatism in the state funding and delivery of welfare, cultural and community services; and (3) significant *fourth industrial revolution* disruptions and transformations in the nature of work, a shift that has disproportionately affected young people globally in terms of their access to employment and education opportunities.

Keywords Art · Social enterprise · Forces of marginalisation · Creative industries · Young creatives · Employment · Education and training

This book explores the opportunities and challenges faced by art-based social enterprises (ASEs) in engaging young people in education and training and supporting their pathways to employment.[1] It also explores the dynamics and implications of 'enterprising' artistic practice for these and other social purposes. This study is thus set against the backdrop of what is termed the *social turn* in contemporary art, in which mainstream artistic practices have become more engaged with the lives of people and communities and with a spirit of collectivism aimed at addressing a range of issues from social exclusion to climate change. This social turn is not, in itself, new—and draws upon histories and traditions of collectivism in arts and cultural practices across the globe and historically. What is new is the ways in which these more social and collective practices have infiltrated the more hierarchical and market-driven aspects of the contemporary art world. In addition, the study is set against the backdrop of rapid growth in social enterprise models across a range of sectors, including the creative industries. This is a growth spurred, in part, by increasing economic pragmatism in the state funding and delivery of welfare, cultural and community services. Finally, this study has taken place in the context of significant 'fourth industrial revolution' disruptions and transformations in the nature of work, a shift that has disproportionately affected young people globally in terms of their access to employment and education opportunities (Neufeind et al., 2018; Panth & Maclean, 2020).

Living with uncertain work futures and amid a climate of work precarity has become increasingly normal for young people in OECD countries in the wake of the 2008–2009 global financial crisis (GFC) (BSL, 2014, Kelly et al., 2015, Standing, 2011). A decade later, the

---

[1] In using the term 'art-based social enterprise', we are advocating for a broad understanding of art that includes diverse media and practices and one that appeals to a cross-section of communities. We recognise the different uses of the terms 'art-based' and 'arts-based' in relation to creative research methods and have elected to use the term 'art-based' with a view to plurality in how we understand 'art.'

unfolding impacts of the COVID-19 pandemic have heightened this atmosphere (and reality) of uncertainty: lockdowns, border closures and social services in crisis have all impacted significantly on opportunities for work generally, and the security of work more specifically. These pandemic impacts have been particularly felt in the creative and cultural industries, fields already subject to precarity in the form of contract work, freelancing and widespread self-employment (Throsby & Petetskaya, 2017; UNESCO, 2021b). The impact of lockdowns in the arts and creative industries in Australia and elsewhere has been significant, resulting in the closure of traditional arts venues such as theatres, galleries and museums, along with the cancellation of large and small festivals, biennales and events—all of these spaces and activities proving difficult to successfully shift online (Commonwealth of Australia, 2021; Eltham & Pennington, 2021). As UNESCO reported in response to the impacts of the pandemic: 'COVID-19 has exposed pre-existing vulnerabilities within the culture sector. Owing to its heavy reliance on venues and shared experiences, the sector has been among the hardest hit by COVID-19' (UNESCO, 2021b).

Alongside this impact on the creative industries, young people have also been disproportionately affected by the pandemic. While some young people have responded to uncertainty by staying in education to effectively 'shelter' from the precarious job market (Witteveen, 2021), those facing barriers to education (in particular young people with experiences of mental health vulnerabilities and learning difficulties, insecure housing and/or language barriers) have been doubly impacted: unable to find work while disengaged from mainstream education and training (OECD, 2021). The numbers of young people in this predicament are surprising and concerning. Responding in part to the impacts of COVID-19, the United Nations reports:

> In 2019, more than one in five of the world's young people were not in employment, education or training, a proportion almost unchanged since 2005. Quarterly figures indicate that the rate increased from the fourth quarter of 2019 to the second quarter of 2020 in 42 out of 49 countries and territories with data. (O'Higgins, 2020)

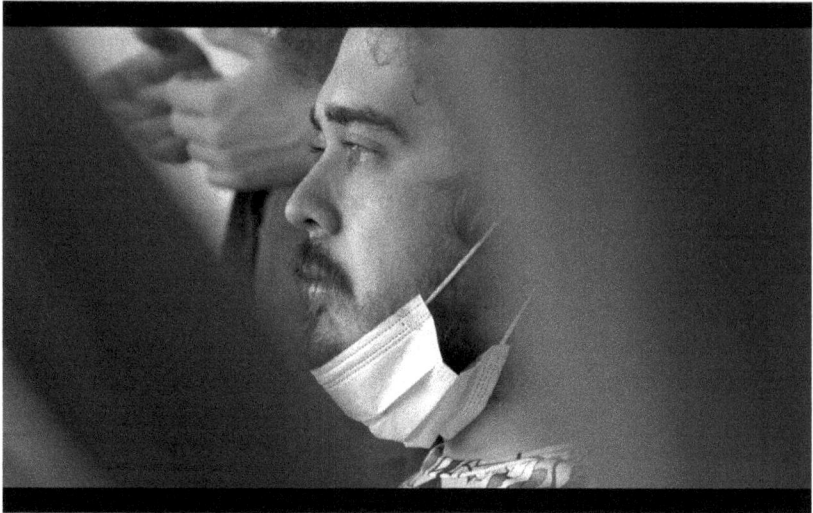

Fig. 1.1 A still from *Emerging* (2020), a video made by students of Youthworx, a media production social enterprise based in Melbourne (Image courtesy of the artists and Youthworx)

Meanwhile, youth unemployment rose in nearly all OECD countries in 2020–2021 (OECD, 2021).

It is in this context that ASEs offer the potential to support young people impacted by global economic conditions and crises, especially in terms of re-engaging them with education and providing pathways to employment (Fig. 1.1). This potential applies to both young people *generally* and those experiencing socio-economic disadvantage more specifically. This is to caution against reducing the activity of ASEs to addressing marginality alone and to insist that the term 'marginalisation' can itself be ambiguous, offensive and even damaging in its use. As we will discuss in further detail later in this chapter, we resist the tendency to associate structural marginalisation with individual identities—which often leads to deficit constructions. Instead, we privilege the skills, talents, interests and voices of young artists engaged in ASEs and understand that they are not in themselves marginal—but are *impacted by* forces of marginalisation. This humanising methodological strategy responds to Eve Tuck's (2009) call to arms for researchers to move away from damage-focused research in the context of social, political and ethnic/racial marginalisation, and towards more emancipatory research frameworks. In the USA, scholars working in this space often prefer the term 'minoritised' to speak to the impacts of marginalisation on communities and shift the emphasis away from supposedly 'damaged' individual identity (Ngo et al., 2017).

In this book, we discuss the forces of marginalisation in relation to social enterprise and in so doing follow in the footsteps of Jessica Gerrard's (2017) *Precarious Enterprise on the Margins: Work, Poverty, and Homelessness in the City*, where she argues for a shift away from the deficit-oriented focus on an individual's experience of marginalisation to instead focus on the social/structural forces driving that marginalisation:

> To write about marginality, therefore, is not a simple undertaking of pointing out and putting under the microscope the experience of marginality. There is a need to address the social dynamics that create such marginality, including the ways in which research can replicate representations of the dysfunctional and marginal 'other'. (Gerrard 2017, p. 27)

We bring this structural critique of marginalisation into this book in two distinct methodological ways: one interpretative and the other participatory. Firstly, while recognising the play of forces that produce marginalisation structurally, we privilege, as noted above, the individual experiences of young people involved in ASEs through the lens of their creativity and attitudes to work, their sense of the creative industries they want to become part of and their vision of a future—thereby de-emphasising disempowering stories of hardship and personal struggle. Secondly, we have worked alongside young artists from our three case study organisations in Melbourne, Australia—Youthworx, The Social Studio and Outer Urban Projects—to co-produce creative works that are woven through the book both in the form of anecdotes and also in selected images. We discuss this further in the methodology and chapter outline section later in this introduction. For the moment, we turn to a discussion of the creative industries, social enterprise and young people living with the forces of marginalisation.

Why the Arts and Creative Industries?

There is an increasing acceptance of the links between creativity, culture and sustainable development—including economic and social development—worldwide, partly driven by UNESCO's global policy advocacy (UNESCO, 2013, 2021b). Yet the potential social, cultural and economic contribution of arts-based enterprise, especially social enterprise, is under-recognised and underutilised (McQuilten et al., 2020; McRobbie, 2011). Work Integration Social Enterprises (WISE) often tend to focus on entry-level employment opportunities in service industries—hospitality, cleaning, caring, building and construction, etc.,—in careers which suit individuals who are already work-motivated and relatively engaged (Kelly et al., 2015). This is less useful for a range of young people who may be more creatively inclined, and particularly for those experiencing marginality and disengagement from education and employment. As Polly, an ASE staff member explained to us during the course of this study:

> I've had three or four people who tell me their job service provider has recommended they go and do Cert III in Childcare because that's where the jobs are but they don't want to do that. They want to produce music or make YouTube videos. So we are offering something that isn't as widely out there but there is a lot of interest and passion in.

What this demonstrates is that for young people, engagement is a central factor in participation in both education and work (Cummings & Blatherwick, 2017). Creativity, as is evidenced throughout this study, provides a powerful means of engagement. The act of creating, making and producing engenders active participation and builds on existing cultural and creative interests—and therefore can play a more significant role in supporting pathways to education and employment, particularly for youth who are already disengaged (Montgomery, 2017).

The creative industries, meanwhile, are growing rapidly, and creative industry training is becoming increasingly diverse. In recognition of this growth, the UN declared 2021 the *International Year of Creativity Economy*. Outlining the importance of the creative industries in driving economic and social development, a UNESCO Roadmap (2021a) reported:

> At the heart of the creative economy are cultural and creative industries (CCIs), which operate at the crossroad of arts, culture, commerce and technology. CCIs generate 2,250 billion USD annually and employ around 30 million people worldwide. They are also the biggest job providers for workers aged 18-25, making it the industry of tomorrow.

Indeed, training in the creative industries involves the development of a range of transferable skills in communication, design, management and innovation. While the contract-based, short-term and precarious nature of creative industries is destabilising (and presents somewhat of a paradox for ASEs in their brief to provide employment pathways), it also mirrors the general pattern of contemporary work in the wake of the 'fourth industrial revolution'—and arguably, helps prepare young people for the kind of entrepreneurial skills required to work across industries. Moreover, as feminist cultural theorist and researcher of creative economy and labour markets Angela McRobbie argues, alongside the values of income security, creatives are also seeking out careers that are fulfilling and meaningful—which may involve lower incomes but better lifestyle and wellbeing (2016).

In this book, as a way of emphasising this diversity and flexibility of arts training, we look at three different sectors within the creative industries, each with different career pathways—digital media production (Youthworx), fashion and textiles design and manufacture (The Social Studio) and performing arts (Outer Urban Projects). These specific areas within the arts support the development of a range of skills. Digital media lends itself to storytelling, social media engagement, multimedia content production, design, communications and marketing; while fashion builds knowledge of design, retail, styling and photography; and the performing arts develops skills in public speaking and presenting, teaching and 'gigging' or managing multiple simultaneous job opportunities. These diverse media thus involve different skills and attract different cohorts of young people. What they share, however, is the capacity to develop more general creative, twenty-first-century skills such as problem-solving, flexibility, perseverance and cooperation that enable pathways from ASEs into a range of industries (Lamb et al., 2015).

Why Social Enterprise?

The social enterprise model, which brings together entrepreneurialism and market-based activity with social goals, is an appealing framework for engaging young people in creative education and training for several reasons. Firstly, social enterprise is driven by an ethos that at least promises to support greater economic independence, sustainability and viability for sectors that have historically been reliant on government funding: a source of income that is generally declining in favour of private-sector, market-based solutions (Denny & Seddon, 2013). This makes social enterprise both reactive (and even acquiescent) to a neoliberalism and potentially also formative of alternative ways of performing a range of economic and social functions—producing, distributing and consuming, employing and training, service provision and community building. As such, social enterprise is one response to a specific kind of funding crisis in the arts and cultural sectors especially, which have historically not been profit-generating, entrepreneurial or financially self-sufficient—an issue that is intricately linked with artistic values of freedom and critique. The old maxim of 'art for art's sake' speaks strongly to these values. Originally, the phrase was a radical concept in the nineteenth century that was embraced by Parisian writers such as Théophile Gautier and Charles Baudelaire to reject the formal association of art with interests of the academy, religion and the state, and has since become synonymous with ideals of artistic freedom (Morgan, 2013). This value of 'art for art's sake' always, in fact, dodged the reality of art as long entwined with patronage and markets—and has increasingly come under threat by the neoliberal economic transformations of the twentieth and twenty-first centuries (Haiven, 2018; Lee Wong, 2018; McQuilten & White, 2016). Simultaneously, there has been a drive towards greater and more direct social engagement from artists disenfranchised by the commercialisation of art and disenchanted with the loss of its socially transformative potential (Bishop, 2006; Sholette & Bass, 2018).

While the rise of ASEs don't solve these tensions, they do offer arts organisations possible models for greater economic viability that also privilege social and artistic goals. Beyond these organisational advantages in the arts sector, ASEs, in particular, offer specific attractions for young people, relating to organisational ethos, scale, flexibility and emplacement in communities and networks. They can offer the ability to engage young people in education and training that is directly related to industry pathways and employability. Learning takes place in a context that is strongly connected to 'real-world' activity, is alternative to mainstream educational settings, revolves around practical and skill-based curriculum and takes place in an environment that provides both work experience and the potential to find work (at best) or generate some income (at least). Social enterprises that operate in the arts and cultural sectors can be of further attraction to young people through tapping into youth cultures, offering a means to explore and express identity, and using creativity to build up both practical, 'hard skills' such as video production or sewing and 'soft skills' that are beneficial for employment across a range of industries such as communication, storytelling, adaptability and problem-solving.

While there is interest and investment in ASEs internationally, there remains large gaps in understanding the nuanced mechanisms through which they operate. This reflects a broader lack of critically informed research on the social enterprise phenomenon per se—with available research coming mainly from the field of business management. Indeed, there is a comparative dearth of research addressing the cultural, social and non-economic dimensions of social enterprise, with only scattered studies drawing on sociological and political economy approaches now emerging (Farmer et al., 2021; Lanctôt et al., 2012; Qian et al., 2019). This research gap has resulted in an over-representation of perspectives that privilege the economic and technocratic aspects of social entrepreneurship and that downplay the complex socio-cultural impact and lived dimensions of designing, operating and using social enterprise models (Dacin et al., 2011).

This is especially pronounced when it comes to understanding ASEs and how those enterprises that focus on youth, in particular, engage, work with and support young people into further education and training. What is clearly evident is that these ASEs face overlapping and distinct sets of aspirations and challenges in redressing the effects of neoliberal capitalism on young people. They navigate similar common tensions, particularly in meeting the need to generate profits to fund activities, achieve social objectives and negotiate complex relationships with multiple stakeholders (Kerlin, 2010). Along with other youth-oriented programs, they are also often resisting and potentially transforming conventional understandings of 'youth transitions' (Kelly et al., 2019).

With this complexity in mind, this study analyses the challenges and opportunities faced by ASEs working with young people in the context of specific art forms and specific socio-economic and cultural contexts in Australia. Drawing on extensive fieldwork and interviews with twelve key organisations, and the three case study organisations mentioned previously (Youthworx, The Social Studio and Outer Urban Projects), the book offers a narrative account of using art-based social enterprise to engage young people in education, training and employment. In doing so, we focus on the specific tensions encountered in social enterprises that use arts-based strategies to engage young people and we provide insights into the lived experience of those involved in ASEs, including staff, students and their communities.

Understanding the perspectives of both staff and students involved in ASEs sheds light on the benefits and opportunities of social enterprise in addressing complex social and economic challenges. It also sheds light on the challenges, paradoxes and complexities of operating organisations that juggle competing goals. This suggests various, interconnected lines of questioning in relation to ASEs. What types of creativity are appealing to young people engaging with these ASEs and why? What do their creative practices tell us about their experiences in a rapidly changing world with multiple, simultaneous global crises (environmental, economic, public health?) Are such pathways into employment realistic and achievable for young people hoping to enter the creative industries? How do ASE staff negotiate the complexity of supporting social outcomes while also pursuing business growth and development?

How does the overtly economic, and arguably neoliberal, motivations of ASEs impact on artistic values such as creative freedom and criticality? What kinds of subjectivities are produced and are emerging for young people engaged with ASEs? All of these questions are explored in the chapters that follow.

Social Enterprise, Marginality and Markets

Over the past few decades, a social enterprise-based approach to providing training and employment pathways for young people has promised to 'break the cycle of youth unemployment' (Campbell et al., 2020). It is well documented that young people have been disproportionately affected by unemployment, underemployment and precarious employment in many OECD economies since the GFC. Moreover, the unfolding global impacts of COVID-19 will, as we noted above, undoubtedly have exacerbated these inequalities. ASEs, in particular, are considered to be highly effective at engaging young people impacted by forces of marginalisation because of their emphasis on learning through expressive and material practice rather than formal knowledge acquisition (McQuilten, 2017; Padovani & Whittaker, 2017).

As we have noted, a key focus of many Work Integration Social Enterprises is the provision of employment and educational pathways for people experiencing forms of social exclusion or economic disadvantage. Yet with this focus comes the challenge of how to support social and economic advancement for affected communities without perpetuating stigma and inadvertently reinforcing those positions of disadvantage (Ngo et al., 2017). If young people are recruited into ASEs on the basis of their relative (individual) experience of being on the margins, for example, how can they exceed that positionality in their educational and work journeys through and beyond the social enterprise programs? As flagged earlier in this chapter, marginalisation—especially in a neoliberal world—is not an issue for the individual; it is produced by structural forces of social exclusion and inequitable economic growth. Yet the forces of neoliberalism, which have brought the decline of the welfare state and rise of privatised welfare solutions, continually reduce marginalisation to an individual, rather than collective, status. As Elyse Gordon argues in her analysis of youth empowerment programs in the USA: '[These] individual level discourses exemplify residual poverty discourses that blames individuals, rather than situating their struggles in relation to structural inequalities such as racialized, gendered, aged and classed barriers' (2013, p. 113). There is little doubt that the rise of social enterprise has taken place in this context of declining support for the collective provision of social welfare and an increased individualisation of disadvantage.

In this book, our understanding of marginalisation and its impacts on young people draws on a range of empirical studies that privilege lived experience from the fields of youth studies, education, community arts and sociology and from emergent literature in social enterprise. We build on this literature to interpret and understand marginalisation as both a structural and collective issue, while being characterised by specificity and difference according to cultural, geographic, political and economic contexts. Our three central case studies, for example, work in specific contexts of structural marginalisation: Youthworx work with young people disengaged from schooling, many of whom experience learning difficulties, mental health challenges and/or forms of neurodiversity, and some of whom experience housing insecurity; The Social Studio works with young people in the context of migration and displacement due to the refugee experience; and Outer Urban Projects work with people experiencing spatial or geographic marginalisation, or as sociologists sometimes describe it, living in a 'poor postcode' (Swan, 2005).

Alongside recognising specific contexts, we are also at pains in this study to locate different forms of marginalisation in relation to the specific creative focus and social goals of our three case study organisations. This specificity is important simply because not all ASEs will serve young people equally, given they focus on particular creative forms and frameworks of marginality. As Hampshire and Matthijsse argue in their study of a large-scale youth singing program in the UK called Sing Up, participation and engagement in the creative arts (and, we might add, in different art forms) are markedly different for young people from different socio-economic, cultural and geographic backgrounds (Hampshire & Matthijsse, 2010). Additionally, Wright, John, Allegia and Sheel have noted the need for future research on the impacts of community arts programs for young people that takes into account the specificity of populations of youth and compares the effects of different art forms and the types of participation they might enable (Wright et al., 2006, p. 651). In the three sections of the book that follow, we therefore look at both specific forms of marginality as produced by social and economic systems, and the specific forms of creative practice—creative digital media, fashion & textiles and performing arts, respectively—that are being deployed in different ways to engage with, and potentially transform, these conditions (Fig. 1.2).

How, then, might social enterprise be positioned to do this? To reiterate key points made already in this introduction, art-based social enterprises sit at the nexus of community development and creative industries and, as a result, they navigate complex territory that includes tensions between social and artistic agendas, on the one hand, and economic and neoliberal forces, on the other (McQuilten et al., 2020). They also offer, as we have emphasised already, extraordinary opportunities for engaging young people in education and work pathways, building on existing interests, skills and talents—a strength-based, rather than deficit-based starting point for engagement. As many scholars across the fields of youth studies and community arts observe, arts engagement programs for young people can build cultural citizenship and enable the development of critical thinking around questions of positionality, identity and their own relation to contemporary social and economic forces (Dickens & Lonie, 2013; Duncombe, 2007; Hickey-Moody, 2010). This potential is counterbalanced by ASEs' own needs to survive in challenging market conditions, drawing together hybrid forms of income from business activities, philanthropy, community and government. As a result, those working in ASEs often demonstrate deep ambivalence towards their entrepreneurial goals—seeing potential for greater independence from government dictates and philanthropic trends, while also facing frustration in having to compromise social and creative goals to expand their commercial operations, reach mainstream audiences and please funders. As Jean, an ASE manager we interviewed explained:

Fig. 1.2 Emerging fashion designer, Nancy Oziya, at work at The Social Studio, a fashion-based social enterprise in Melbourne (Photograph: Teva Cosic)

> I think that social enterprises can be pushed into, grow-grow-grow-grow-grow, and we're taking the time to go, actually let's really sensibly sit and pause for a minute – we might not necessarily grow in scope, but we can dig deeper on our social impact, for example, or we could get better at our businesses and so that they contribute more financially. (Jean)

Young people involved in ASEs face a similar tension: developing skills and capability in the arts can be empowering, and yet realistic pathways into the creative industries are vexed—careers are precarious, often atomised, and incomes are notoriously low (Bridgstock, 2013; Throsby & Petetskaya, 2017). This is particularly challenging for young people from lower socio-economic backgrounds and from communities where their economic and social situation can mean that they need to find careers which are pragmatic and can support economic advancement over creative expression (Oppedal et al., 2017). Morgan and Idriss (2012) explain this dilemma between pursuing artistic goals and economic goals for young creatives from middle class, Arabic-speaking backgrounds in Sydney, Australia:

> The projects of social mobility are complicated not only by the challenge of translating often precarious and unconventional vocational choices across linguistic and cultural divides, but also in explaining to those who have long been employed in 'old economy' jobs how the contemporary vocational landscape has changed. Nevertheless, each of our interviewees has sacrificed the pursuit of artistic purity, abandoned the idea of complete creative fulfilment, in the face of the practical challenges of earning a living. (p. 941)

ASEs, then, are a complex terrain. They bring together learning opportunities, creative exploration and expression, active citizenship and potential pathways to employment and income generation for the young people who engage with them, but those young people still must contend with the exigencies of labour markets and career choice. Likewise, those who run ASEs must contend with the funding and market environments in which they operate.

It is in this sense that the entrepreneurial drive of ASEs can be seen to be both complicit with the forces of neoliberalism while also offering a means to work within the constraints of neoliberal conditions to forge pathways that enable difference and activate social and economic opportunity for marginalised communities. A number of scholars who write on art and enterprise have argued for an engagement with economic systems that reconfigure, renegotiate and transform economic organisation to better support artists and artistic work (Lee Wong, 2019; McRobbie, 2011). Ashley Lee Wong, for example, has explained that 'the politics here is not one of questioning existing systems, but finding a means to operate within market economies to regain forms of agency' (2019). What is being advocated then is a politics that is pragmatic and affirmative in response to the dominance of neoliberalism: a possibility of working productively within systems in order to carve out economic and creative autonomy while dealing with the reality that young creatives must find opportunities to obtain meaningful paid work.

More broadly, this articulates with the work of a number of scholars who contest an entrenched 'radical' critique of market participation and advocate a shift to a flexible understanding of 'challenging capitalism'. There has been a discernible shift away from a sense of markets as a priori de-socialising and de-politicising—suggesting instead a reading of markets as involving a field of agential entities that continually shape, enact and configure what the economic is and can be (Cochoy et al., 2016). Similarly, in imagining a post-capitalism, Katherine Gibson and Julie Graham take issue with a habit of thinking on the left that, in looking always to a thorough transformation of economy, leaves no room for the generous recognition of current alternative economic practices that unsettle the assumed ubiquity of neoliberal capitalism and represent a possibility of difference through local transformation (Gibson-Graham, 2006a, 2006b). Here, local, micropolitical interventions—from cooperatives and not-for-profits to ethical and social enterprises—gesture towards new ontologies in the larger, political realm—what might be considered new performances of economy (Gibson-Graham, 2006a: 79; see also Gibson-Graham et al., 2013; Humphery, 2017). In the case of ASEs, this also clearly entails new performances of education and training.

These possibilities are perhaps especially characteristic of the creative realm. Angela McRobbie advocates for what she terms 'radical social enterprise' that mobilises self-organised collectives and cooperatives as a response to changing work and welfare conditions. She notes that 'already many artists and creative people are working in communities and on social projects' and she speculates that there is scope in the expansion of such radical 'strategies for social cooperation' (McRobbie, 2011, p. 33). In her more recent book, *Be Creative* (2016), McRobbie observes an emergence of social and creative entrepreneurship in the cultural sector which urgently addresses the question of how to 'finance activities that in the past were part of the public sector' (p. 4). She cautions against dismissing entrepreneurial culture as merely a product of neoliberal capitalism. Indeed, McRobbie insists that participating in market economy is no longer a choice, but 'necessary for survival' and has the potential to support creative livelihoods, income streams and job creation, and even to develop new forms of community building and cultural economy (McRobbie, 2016, p. 4).

Our research adds to this discourse by presenting detailed insights into the mechanisms of this 'engagement with' market forces in order to generate social and cultural (rather than economic) gains. ASEs, as we have noted, so often inhabit a dual position of being simultaneously affirming and critical of the profit-driven contemporary economic landscape, with aspirations (not always fulfilled) to challenge and transform mainstream business in ways that can address structural inequalities. As Miriam, an ASE manager explained to us:

> Addressing marginalisation is not so much about addressing the subject who is marginalised, but addressing [the] mainstream to let the subject in, you know. Stop pushing people away […] we understand how [the] market does that and we're trying to reshape it a little.

Sometimes that 'little' can mean a lot, as will be seen in the chapters that follow. This study therefore recognises and affirms that there is radical potential for both ASEs and the young people engaged with them to activate markets, education and work in ways that challenge and resist dominant neoliberal logics.

The Study That Follows

This book has been developed out of a five-year, qualitative research project (2017–2022) that brought together scholars across contemporary art, education, youth studies, sociology and the sociology of consumption to explore the benefits of art-based social enterprise for young people experiencing forms of social marginalisation. Addressing key gaps in understanding the lived experience of ASEs, in terms of both their organisational modes of being and the lived experience of young people involved with them, we undertook in-depth fieldwork in three stages. The first stage involved mapping ASEs across Australia, which led to interviews with managing staff from 12 ASEs in order to better understand the opportunities and challenges of the art-based social enterprise model. The second stage of the research involved the detailed case studies of three ASEs in Melbourne already introduced above—Youthworx, The Social Studio and Outer Urban Projects.

A key driver of our methodology in working with young people has been to activate their creative voices in the research itself, and in so doing, to transform the extractive research approach of traditional scholarship (which tends to reinforce a power structure that privileges the academic over their research subjects) by enabling opportunities for exchange. To reiterate, the work of Eve Tuck has been influential here (2009; Tuck & Yang, 2013). In 'Suspending Damage: Letter to Communities' (2009), Tuck discusses the tendency for academic research to see communities through a lens of deficit. In relation to undertaking research with young people impacted by forces of marginalisation, she asked a number of pertinent questions:

> The lives of city youth – already under the watchful eyes of police and school security officers, already tracked by video cameras in their schools, on the streets, and in subways – are pursued by (well-intentioned) researchers whose work functions as yet another layer of surveillance. What will be the outcomes and effects of this research in and on our communities? Are we certain that the benefits will outweigh the costs? What questions might we ask ourselves before we allow researcher entry? (2009, p. 410)

In practice, asking ourselves these questions has meant co-producing exhibitions, performances, talks and events with emerging artists from each of our case study organisations; listening to their perspectives; allowing space for conversation on desires, aspirations and hopes; not asking young people to 'testify' to their personal circumstances and therefore reinforce deficit constructions; allowing total anonymity, where preferred, in order to engender honest and critical conversations;

and supporting ongoing collaboration with creative projects that will continue well beyond the duration of the research project itself (as well as the writing and publishing of this book). It has also meant accepting the choice of young people not to engage in the research or creative projects, and to withdraw from the research where relevant.

Our case studies for this book have therefore involved multiple methods: observation, attendance at public-facing events, participation in creative workshops, interviews with young artists, interviews with staff at regular intervals throughout the project, organisational mapping with managing staff and the co-development of several creative projects with Youthworx, The Social Studio and Outer Urban Projects. These co-produced creative projects are woven into the chapters that follow. They include an exhibition at Bus Projects held from 19 January to 27 February 2021 titled *Joining My Future: Art/Work, Inequality and Crisis*, several weaving workshops with artist Muhubo Sulieman from The Social Studio; a fashion showcase, performances and film screening as part of the Australian Centre for Contemporary Art's major exhibition *Who's Afraid of Public Space?* (2021–2022); and a podcast produced by Crawl Space Radio & Bus Projects (Fig. 1.3). As this is a book about art practice, we have privileged, throughout our analysis, the material and embodied nature of 'making' in the research.

We have also attended to the challenges of giving 'voice' to our research participants. The research team was acutely aware of potentially problematic directions in the interviews and collaborations with young people—for example, extracting testimonies of disadvantage, drawing participants into conversations that could trigger past traumatic experiences or reconfirming unequal power dynamics between staff, researchers and young people involved in ASEs. Interviews with young people were therefore developed using a life-grid drawing method (Wilson et al., 2007) that enabled students to direct the conversation loosely around three themes—what led them to being involved in the ASE, their experience at the ASE and their future aspirations. Staff interviews, on the other hand, were semi-structured, utilising a set of open-ended questions directed towards the challenges and opportunities of the ASE model at different points in time.

Fig. 1.3 A still from *Silence, Dance, Poetry* (2020), a video by Outer Urban Projects performing artist Damian Seddon (Image courtesy of the artist and Outer Urban Projects)

Drawing on this broad array of qualitative data, this book is structured around three themes, corresponding to both the broader international context and also the specific conditions of each of our case studies. In Chapters 2 and 3, we turn to the theme of precarious youth and digital futures (Youthworx), documenting the opportunities and challenges that arise when creative digital media training is harnessed to support reengagement in education and training for disengaged youth. We identify a key challenge for ASEs in supporting young people with complex needs and also meeting external pressures to achieve targets in relation to employment transitions, particularly given the precarity of the creative industries. In Chapters 4 and 5, we look at material practice, fashion and textiles and their potential to provide a strength-based training and employment platform for young people who have been impacted by migration and displacement. Engaging with staff and participants at The Social Studio, we identify a tension between aspiration and pragmatism that is expressed both by the art-based social enterprise itself in navigating the fashion industry and also by students who are often tempering their ambitions with a grounded realism. We then move in Chapters 6 and 7 to explore spatialised forms of marginalisation, voice and the performing arts, through drawing on our engagement with Outer Urban Projects. We examine the question of how neoliberal values of entrepreneurship and individual advancement can intersect with collective forms of sociopolitical consciousness, critique and transformation that emerge in performing arts youth programs. Together, these chapters bring critical analysis of the operating models, pedagogical approaches and impacts of these ASEs with a narrative exploration of the everyday experience of staff, students and young artists involved. We thus draw on rich data throughout the chapters—gathered through interviews, ethnographic observations and organisational analyses—in order to provide insights into an expanding ASE sector that is attracting widespread interest.

Finally, Chapter 8 concludes the study by way of synthesising the key themes of aspiration, hope, complexity, ambivalence, resistance and contestation that run throughout this book—and we highlight the ways in which our research points to several under-recognised impacts of ASEs. Firstly, individual engagement in ASEs can lead to collective forms of systemic change—both in terms of how ASEs and the young people involved in them are influencing mainstream industry and in terms of how young people are developing forms of expression that challenge and transform—through acts of cultural democracy and sociopolitical consciousness—dominant hegemonic representations of 'youth' (Dickens & Lonie, 2013; Ngo et al., 2017). Secondly, young people who are subject to marginalising forces may be drawn, by necessity, to more entrepreneurial or 'instrumental' forms of creative engagement, not least because the privileged notion of art for art's sake is not equally available to all young artists. Thirdly, while industry and government look to ASEs to produce quantifiable impacts in terms of employment and educational 'transitions', less recognised (and arguably undervalued) outcomes for young people can be found in improved health and wellbeing, along with the benefits of engagement in itself: social connection, active participation, increased confidence and creative expression (Montgomery, 2017). Finally, a particular role that ASEs are playing for emerging creatives is linking them to broader social and professional 'bridging networks'—crucial for getting ahead in the creative industries, while also broadening opportunities for social and creative connection (Warr, 2006). These outcomes are the essential precursors, we argue, to more quantifiable outcomes including long-term employment and educational journeys (FYA, 2015; Kelly et al., 2019).

Currently, the social enterprise field is dominated by polarised views: critics, on the one hand, and advocates, on the other. This book aims to move the field forward with a critical lens that engages closely with the experience and lived realities of juggling multiple priorities of social, economic and artistic goals. As we ultimately argue in this book, ASEs are offering new, art-based, imaginative and compelling educational programs for young people around the globe, with particular effect in communities impacted by forces of marginalisation. In the cases we study, these educational and creative innovations are developed through a reciprocal collaboration with young artists and their communities.

References

Bishop, C. (2006). The social turn: Collaboration and its discontents. *Artforum International, 44*(6), 178–183.

Bridgstock, R. (2013). Not a dirty word: Arts entrepreneurship and higher education. *Arts and Humanities in Higher Education, 12*(2–3), 122–137.

BSL. (2014). *Youth employment report*. Brotherhood of St Laurence, Melbourne. Accessed 24 August 2021, http://www.bsl.org.au/Advocacy/Youthemployment.aspx

Campbell, P., Carey, G., Farmer, J., Joyce, A., et al. (2020). *Improving health equity among young people: The role of social enterprise. An evidence and practice summary*. Centre for Social Impact Swinburne, Melbourne.

Cochoy, F., Trompette, P., & Araujo, L. (2016). From market agencements to market agencing: An introduction. *Consumption, Markets & Culture, 19*(1), 3–16.

Commonwealth of Australia. (2021). *Sculpting a national cultural plan: Igniting a post-COVID economy for the arts*. Parliament of the Commonwealth of Australia. Accessed 24 January 2022, https://www.aph.gov.au/Parliamentary_Business/Committees/House/Communications/Arts/Report.

Cummings, J., & Blatherwick, M. L. (2017). *Creative dimensions of teaching and learning in the 21st century*. SensePublishers.

Dacin, M. T., Dacin, P. A., & Tracey, P. (2011). Social entrepreneurship: A critique and future directions. *Organization Science, 22*(5), 1203–1213.

Denny, S., & Seddon, F. (Eds.). (2013). *Social enterprise: Accountability and evaluation around the world*. Taylor & Francis Group.

Dickens, L., & Lonie, D. (2013). Rap, rhythm and recognition: Lyrical practices and the politics of voice on a community music project for young people experiencing challenging circumstances. *Emotion, Space and Society, 9*, 59–71.

Duncombe, S. (2007). (From) Cultural resistance to community development. *Community Development Journal, 42*(4), 490–500.

Eltham, B., & Pennington, A. (2021). *Creativity in crisis: Rebooting Australia's arts and entertainment sector after COVID*. The Centre for Future Work, The Australia Institute.

Farmer, J., De Cotta, T., Kilpatrick, S., Barraket, J., et al. (2021). How work integration social enterprises help to realize capability: A comparison of three Australian settings. *Journal of Social Entrepreneurship, 12*(1), 87–109.

FYA. (2015). *How are young people faring in the transition from school to work*. Foundation for Young Australians, Melbourne.

Gerrard, J. (2017). *Precarious enterprise on the margins work, poverty, and homelessness in the city* (1st ed. 2017). Palgrave Macmillan.

Gibson-Graham, J. K., Cameron, J., & Healy, S. (2013). *Take back the economy: An ethical guide for transforming our communities*. University of Minnesota Press.

Gibson-Graham, J. K. (2006a). *A postcapitalist politics*. University of Minnesota Press.

Gibson-Graham, J. K. (2006b). *The end of capitalism (as we knew it): A feminist critique of political economy*. University of Minnesota Press.

Gordon, E. (2013). Under-served and un-deserving: Youth empowerment programs, poverty discourses and subject formation. *Geoforum, 50*, 107–116.

Haiven, M. (2018). *Art after money, money after art*. Pluto Press.

Hampshire, K., & Matthijsse, M. (2010). Can arts projects improve young people's wellbeing? A social capital approach. *Social Science & Medicine (1982), 71*(4), 708–716.

Hickey-Moody, A. (2010). Youth arts, place and differential becomings of the world. *Continuum, 24*(2), 203–214.

Humphery, K. (2017). The accidental enterprise: Ethical consumption as commerce. *Geoforum, 85*, 92–100.

Kelly, P. (2006). The entrepreneurial self and youth at-risk: Exploring the horizons of identity in the 21st century. *Journal of Youth Studies, 9*(1), 17–32.

Kelly, P., Campbell, P., & Harrison, L. (2015). "Don't be a smart arse": Social enterprise-based transitional labour-market programmes as neo-liberal technologies of the self. *British Journal of Sociology of Education, 36*(4), 558–576.

Kelly, P., Campbell, P., & Howie, L. (2019). *Rethinking young people's marginalisation: Beyond neo-liberal futures?* Routledge.

Kerlin, J. (2010). A comparative analysis of the global emergence of social enterprise. *Voluntas: International Journal of Voluntary and Nonprofit Organizations, 21*(2), pp. 162–179.

Lamb, S., Jackson, J., & Rumberger, R. (2015). *ISCY technical paper: Measuring 21st century skills in ISCY*. Technical Report. Victoria University, Centre for International Research on Educational Systems, Victoria University, Melbourne, VIC.

Lanctôt, N., Durand, M.-J., & Corbière, M. (2012). The quality of work life of people with severe mental disorders working in social enterprises: A qualitative study. *Quality of Life Research, 21*(8), 1415–1423.

Lee Wong, A. (2018). Artists in the creative economy: Inoperative modes of resistance. *APRJA (A Peer Reviewed Journal About), 7*(1), 115–126.

Lee Wong, A. (2019, Spring). Artists as enterprise: Incorporating as forms of organising agencies. *PARSE Journal, 9*. Accessed January 19 2022, http://parsejournal.com/article/artists-as-enterprise-incorporating-as-forms-of-organising-agencies/

McQuilten, G. (2017). The political possibilities of art and fashion based social enterprise. *Continuum, 31*(1), 69–83.

McQuilten, G., Warr, D., Humphery, K., & Spiers, A. (2020). Ambivalent entrepreneurs: Arts-based social enterprise in a neoliberal world. *Social Enterprise Journal, 16*(2), 121–140.

McQuilten, G., & White, A. (2016). *Art as enterprise: Social and economic engagement in contemporary art*. I.B. Tauris.

McRobbie, A. (2011). Re-thinking creative economy as radical social enterprise. *Variant, 41*, 32–33.

McRobbie, A. (2016). *Be creative: Making a living in the new culture industries*. Polity Press.

Montgomery, D. (2017). The rise of creative youth development. *Arts Education Policy Review, 118*(1), 1–18.

Morgan, G., & Idriss, S. (2012). "Corsages on their parents' jackets": Employment and aspiration among Arabic-speaking youth in Western Sydney. *Journal of Youth Studies, 15*(7), 929–943.

Morgan, H. (2013). Art for art's sake. *Grove Art Online*. Accessed 24 January 2022, https://www.oxfordartonline.com/groveart/view/10.1093/gao/9781884446054.001.0001/oao-9781884446054-e-7000004365

Neufeind, M., O'Reilly, J., & Ranft, F. (2018). *Work in the digital age: Challenges of the fourth industrial revolution*. Policy Network.

Ngo, B., Lewis, C., & Maloney Leaf, B. (2017). Fostering sociopolitical consciousness with minoritized youth: Insights from community-based arts programs. *Review of Research in Education, 41*(1), 358–380.

OECD. (2021, July). *What have countries done to support young people in the COVID-19 crisis?* OECD Policy Responses to Coronavirus (COVID-19). Accessed 18 January 2022, https://www.oecd.org/coronavirus/policy-respon ses/what-have-countries-done-to-support-young-people-in-the-covid-19-cri sis-ac9f056c/

O'Higgins, N. (2020). *Young people not in employment, education or training* (ILO/SIDA Partnership on Employment Technical Brief No. 3). International Labour Organisation. Accessed 15 December 2021.

Oppedal, B., Guribye, E., & Kroger, J. (2017). Vocational identity development among unaccompanied refugee minors. *International Journal of Intercultural Relations, 60*, 145–159.

Padovani, C., & Whittaker, P. (2017). *Sustainability and the social fabric: Europe's new textile industries*. Bloomsbury Publishing.

Panth, B., & Maclean, R. (2020). *Anticipating and preparing for emerging skills and jobs*. Springer Nature.

Qian, J., Riseley, E., & Barraket, J. (2019, August). *Do employment-focused social enterprises provide a pathway out of disadvantage? An evidence review*. Centre for Social Impact, Swinburne University. Accessed January 19 2022, https://apo.org.au/node/251711

Sholette, G., & Bass, C. (Eds.). (2018). *Art as social action: An introduction to the principles and practices of teaching social practice art*. Allworth Press, an Imprint of Skyhorse Publishing.

Standing, G. (2011). *The precariat: The new dangerous class*. Bloomsbury Academic.

Swan, W. (2005). *Postcode: The splintering of a nation*. Pluto Press.

Throsby, D., & Petetskaya, K. (2017). *Making art work: An economic study of professional artists in Australia*. Australia Council for the Arts, Strawberry Hills, NSW.

Tuck, E. (2009). Suspending damage: A letter to communities. *Harvard Educational Review, 79*(3), 409–427; 539–540.

Tuck, E., & Yang, K. W. (2013). *Youth resistance research and theories of change.* Taylor and Francis.

UNESCO. (2013). *Creative economy report.* United Nations Educational, Scientific and Cultural Organization. Accessed 15 August 2021, http://www.unesco.org/culture/pdf/creative-economy-report-2013.pdf

UNESCO. (2021a). *Roadmap: International year of creative economy for sustainable development.* United Nations Educational, Scientific and Cultural Organization. Accessed 3 January 2022, https://en.unesco.org/sites/default/files/creative_economy2021-unesco-roadmapen-ok2.pdf

UNESCO. (2021b, January). *The tracker: Culture and public policy.* Issue 5. Accessed 19 January 2022, https://en.unesco.org/news/tracker-culture-public-policy-issue-5

Warr, D. (2006). Gender, class, and the art and craft of social capital. *Sociological Quarterly, 47*(3), 497–520.

Wilson, S., Cunningham-Burley, S., Bancroft, A., Backett-Milburn, K., & Masters, H. (2007). Young people, biographical narratives and the life grid: Young people's accounts of parental substance use. *Qualitative Research: QR, 7*(1), 135–151.

Witteveen, D. (2021). Encouraged or discouraged? The effect of adverse macroeconomic conditions on school leaving and reentry. *Sociology of Education, 94*(2), 103–123.

Wright, R., John, L., Alaggia, R., & Sheel, J. (2006). Community-based arts program for youth in low-income communities: A multi-method evaluation. *Child & Adolescent Social Work Journal, 23*(5), 635–652.

2

Precarious Youth and Digital Futures

Abstract This chapter explores the ways in which young creatives who are training and working in the fields of media and digital production are developing skills for the 'workplace of the future.' In the context of art-based social enterprises (ASEs), creative digital media skills offer an exciting means to bridge the gap between disengaged young people and education specifically, with further opportunities for pathways to employment. This chapter explores the challenges and often intangible benefits of working in media spaces with young people experiencing barriers to education, and weighs these challenges and benefits against the expectation that ASEs achieve quantifiable goals in terms of youth transitions into employment. In order to support the inclusion of diverse cohorts of young people in digital media education, the social enterprise model offers the potential to address access issues and engage a range of young people more meaningfully in digital media training. Notwithstanding this fact, social enterprise organisations offering potential employment pathways into the digital media industries face complexities, including the precarious nature of the media industry itself: most work is contract-based, short term, and subject to extreme market fluctuations, most evident in the impacts of COVID-19 lockdowns.

Keywords Digital media · Creative industries · Young creatives · Employment · Education · Youth transitions · Precarity

Introduction: From Disengagement to the Digital

This chapter explores the ways in which young people who are training and working in the fields of media and digital production are developing skills for the 'workplace of the future'. In the context of ASEs, creative digital media skills offer an exciting means to bridge the gap between disengaged young people and education specifically, with further opportunities for pathways to employment. This chapter explores the challenges and often intangible benefits of working in media spaces with young people experiencing barriers to education, and weighs these challenges and benefits against the expectation that art-based social enterprises (ASEs) achieve quantifiable goals in terms of youth transitions into employment.

In the context of the ongoing global challenges of youth unemployment and higher levels of youth disengagement from education and training, creative media programs are seen as offering an effective alternative career pathway, with the potential to re-engage young people in learning and connect them to employment programs (Dowmunt et al., 2007). Globally, the levels of young people aged 15–24 who are not in employment, education or training (NEET) have been persistently, if stagnantly, high. According to the International Labour Organisation's 2020 statistics, this number was 22.4%, more than one in five (O'Higgins, 2020). Youth NEET is not a homogenous group, and in fact, the specific contexts for disengagement are widely different according to geographic and social context. Certain characteristics are associated with higher levels of NEET in OECD countries, including disability, parental education and gender (Kevelson et al., 2020). Meanwhile, young people across cultural and geographic borders are almost universally engaged with creative media through patterns of digital cultural consumption, from watching Tik Tok videos to listening to music on Spotify.

Increasingly, it is becoming easier to produce digital media content through apps and accessible programs without the need for specialised skills or technical know-how. Appetites are increasing for low-fi media content which is accessible to diverse audiences and able to be produced without the need for high-level technical skills. Termed 'internet ugly' by Nick Douglas (2014), the particular aesthetics of amateur production are not a sign of poor quality in contemporary digital media cultures, but in fact a sign of the internet's ubiquity, accessibility and creative freedom. As Douglas writes:

> Internet Ugly, although not the only core aesthetic of the internet, is the one that best defines the internet against all other media. It is certainly the core aesthetic of memetic internet content. The ugliness of the amateur internet doesn't destroy its credibility because it's a byproduct of the medium's advantages (speed and lack of gatekeepers), and even its visual accidents are prized by its most avid users and creators. (2014, p. 315)

The rise of the bedroom YouTube star is evidence of the potential for amateurs to develop the skills to not only produce creative digital content, but also profit from it. The accessibility and creativity of digital media are especially relevant for young people who may lack confidence in a classroom environment. Engaging with digital media and creating short videos, recordings and animations can provide active and empowering ways to learn. Creative media forms thus lend themselves to developing literacy and communication skills as well as transferable skills for employment—entrepreneurial and other twenty-first-century skills and competencies, such as initiative, perseverance, adaptability, cooperation and creative thinking that are important precursors for attaining employment and succeeding in workplaces of the future (Lamb et al., 2015).

Indeed, digital media is increasingly seen as a key industry of the future across workplaces, and creative digital media skills are now understood to be crucial to the survival of the creative and cultural industries: 'Digitalization has been a gamechanger for the creative economy, impacting the entire creative value chain and changing the way we communicate, create and work' (UNESCO, 2021). The ability to create content for social media and websites is a skill in hot demand, and therefore, digital media also offers the potential to carve out career pathways for young people developing these skills. The phenomenon of 'Digital Storytelling' has become a genre in and of itself: on the one hand as a medium for the empowerment of diverse community perspectives through the creation of simple video-based stories drawing on personal experience and, on the other, as a powerful marketing tool for engaging audiences and, ultimately, selling products (Dunford & Jenkins, 2018; Nicoli et al., 2021). This somewhat contradictory, dual function of digital storytelling (community building and brand building) is evident when communications theorists Nicoli et al. (2021) write:

> Digitalisation of storytelling is offered as a means to address fundamental problems in contemporary democratic societies. Citizens can tell their story, engage with supporters and connect people to digital information at all hours of the day [...] Brands can use DST approaches to establish a stronger, more immersive experience with the consumer. (n.p.)

Training in digital media also offers the promise of addressing future crises of employment brought about by automation and artificial intelligence, a threat to traditions of manual and physical labour, by offering the development of skills for future jobs 'that haven't yet been invented' (Ford, 2015; Gregory et al., 2019). It is worth noting, however, that fear of human redundancy is potentially overplayed in contemporary media discourses, and that the likelihood is that new industries developing out of automation and AI will just as likely create jobs as usurp them (Dahlin, 2019). Nevertheless, for young people experiencing unemployment, traditional pathways to work through manual skills-based training (e.g. apprenticeships in trades) may be less appealing in the context of these changes to the nature of work in the twenty-first century, while skills and training in creative digital media are appealing both in their engagement with youth cultures and in this alignment with future-oriented workscapes.

Worldwide, there is significant interest in linking youth unemployment with creative digital media programs, and this is evident in literature that documents and evaluates youth media programs in terms of both wellbeing outcomes and employment and educational pathways (Dowmunt et al., 2007). A report by Chandler et al. (2012) for the Media Trust in the UK demonstrates this broader international enthusiasm, advocating for the relationship between youth media training and practical skills development for employment:

> Youth media is a particularly effective tool for engaging young people from the widest range of backgrounds. The combination of technical, educational, social, creative and investigative practices makes media activity an exciting process – even more so as the end result can be communicated to an audience [...] In an age of on-going mass unemployment, youth media is one vehicle to provide people with the skills needed for employment. (p. 8)

Forms of digital media that have been utilised for youth engagement and training programs span the use of traditional media such as radio and video to expanded media such as digital photography, animation and games. Importantly, digital media enables the development of a range of creative skills including visualisation, storytelling and expression. Perhaps most significantly in the literature, engagement with media is seen to give young people voice and to afford social and political agency, with the potential to challenge problematic constructions of identity or community, to reclaim positive expressions of culture and identity and to find a community of peers with similar interests (Leeuw & Rydin, 2007; Poole, 2010; Steinkuehler & King, 2009). This is of particular interest for young creatives impacted by cultural and socio-economic marginalisation, where the potential for social and political engagement meets values of inclusion and improved wellbeing (Soep, 2006).

This highlights a key issue for ASEs working in digital media. While industry training in the digital media field presents as one solution to youth unemployment, there are access issues that also need to be considered. Firstly, there are practical questions of access to technology. Computers, tablets and smartphones are expensive and require regular upgrades, while internet access is dependent on financial resources to purchase data and geographic access to networks—which can be particularly challenging when working with larger digital media platforms including those dependent on large downloads/uploads. In Australia, for example, key determinants for digital exclusion have been found to be income, employment and education (Borg & Smith, 2018). Secondly, there are complex dynamics in how digital media is used by different demographic and socio-economic groups. In *Teen Mental Health in an Online World*, Betton and Woollard (2018) discuss the ways in which young people with lower levels of education, living with disability and/or from poorer socio-economic backgrounds are less likely to be active producers of media content, and more likely to lack digital literacy skills, resulting in a tendency towards more passive forms of cultural consumption. They write: 'Digital exclusion is not only about access to digital technologies and broadband, but is also about having the skills, motivation and confidence to use the internet in order to participate in society' (p. 123).

In order to support the inclusion of diverse cohorts of young people in digital media education, the social enterprise model, as this and other studies suggest, offers the potential to address these access issues and engage a range of young people more meaningfully in digital media training (Rennie & Podkalicka, 2014). Creativity and alternative economic models go hand in hand and, increasingly, social innovation and social enterprise discourses are recognising the potential of creative industries to engage communities and support sustainable approaches to addressing social problems (Gregory et al., 2019). While SEs are often under-resourced and must, like other enterprises, compete in markets in order to generate income, their emphasis on process as much, if not more so than profit, is a model that can potentially provide additional supports that foster the engagement of target groups experiencing barriers to education and employment (Denny & Seddon, 2013). Notwithstanding this fact, social enterprise organisations offering potential employment pathways into the digital media industries face complexities, not the least of which is the precarious nature of the media industry itself: most work is contract-based, short term, and subject to extreme market fluctuations, most evident recently in the impacts of COVID-19 lockdowns (UNESCO, 2021).

Education and Training Pathways

What, then, can SEs in the creative media industries offer in terms of engaging young people in education and training? The skills developed through creative media programs include 'hard' technical skills such as the use of cameras, lighting and sound recording equipment, useful for gaining working in these specific industries. As discussed above, there is considerable evidence that digital media training can also provide a range of 'soft', twenty-first-century or informal skills that are nevertheless difficult to quantify and formally accredit. These include skills in communication, learning to learn and developing confidence in learning, the ability to tell a story, imagination, expression, problem-solving—and simply being challenged to do something new (Dowmunt et al., 2007; Media Trust, 2012). While these are essential precursors for transitioning into further education and employment, there is still a gap between developing such skills and building careers out of them, specifically in convincing many industries of the value of these competencies and skills to the workforce of the future.

In the light of this, formal accreditation via vocational training and university credit—whether through a mainstream or ASE program—can bring benefits in terms of validating skills acquisition and legitimating employment pathways. However, such accreditation can also be a barrier for several reasons. Firstly, training packages based on vocational skills can be mismatched with creative development and rapid transformations in industry (Jones, 2018). This means that in the digital media industries especially, training packages can quickly become outdated. Secondly, the requirement to achieve certain goals/competencies, along with the linear nature of accreditation, can be ill-suited to the interests and creative approaches of students who have struggled in mainstream schooling (Gidley, 2007). Moreover, the costs of accreditation can be prohibitive to both the organisations that offer it and potential students.

With this in mind, it is important to consider expectations versus reality when it comes to engaging young people in creative media training through ASEs. While creative digital media offers many important entry points for young people to build skills and confidence in learning, gain work experience and potentially access pathways to further education and training, there is an equal likelihood that creative media engagement may become an end-point in and of itself (Rennie & Podkalicka, 2014). In other words, these programs can sometimes provide points of participation, but not necessarily employment or higher educational pathways, especially since young people experiencing disengagement from schooling due to mental health, learning and socio-economic challenges require substantial (and costly) supports for ongoing involvement in education and training, and similarly employment, that are simply not available in mainstream contexts (McGregor & Mills, 2012).

A key function of ASEs that can address this gap between engagement in training and further pathways beyond engagement is in developing social and professional networks for young artists. In 'Gender, Class and the Art and Craft of Social Capital' (2006), Deborah Warr describes the important role of both 'bonding networks' and 'bridging networks' in supporting the development of opportunities for people living in lower socio-economic demographics. In her analysis, she offers a critique of traditional discourses around social capital, which tend not to take into consideration the impacts of class, gender and disadvantage in the potential for individuals and communities to deploy their social capital. Bonding networks speak to the important relational links between people with their families, relatives and friends, often with similar life experiences and identities, while bridging networks speak to more disparate links to people, workplaces and communities that are less supportive, but offer more opportunities to extend out from a particular neighbourhood and set of circumstances—for example to access work opportunities—and to break free from geographic and socio-economic limitations. Warr writes, 'bridging networks are important social structures for facilitating heterogeneous social contacts and new opportunities, and for circulating fresh ideas and information', which can provide a means of 'getting ahead' (2006, pp. 502, 503).

Increased engagement and wellbeing, along with the formation of bridging networks, are therefore significant outcomes that should not be undervalued, particularly in the context of youth wellbeing—despite the fact that international policy tends to focus on quantifiable measures of employment 'transitions' as a measure of success. Youth studies scholar Andy Furlong (2015) cautions against such an approach, arguing 'The problem is that a quantitative focus on transitions often reveals patterns while leaving us relatively unenlightened about the long-term processes that lead to these patterns' (p. 18). Instead, he advocates for a more holistic approach to understanding youth transitions that accounts for lived experience and cultural context—an approach that informs this book.

Opportunities and Challenges of Digital Environments

ASEs in the media space also contend with broader dynamics of digital communication. Digital media as a field not only has issues in terms of inclusion and access, but social media and internet discourses can also have profoundly detrimental effects on the mental health and wellbeing of young people. An OECD study of young people's internet usage, for example, found that young people who spent over six hours a day online (beyond school hours) were more likely to report feelings of loneliness and life dissatisfaction (OECD, 2018). The same study pointed to the significant impacts of cyberbullying on mental health and wellbeing for young people (OECD, 2018).

Social enterprises operating in the digital media training field need to equip their students and staff with a range of skills to mediate these negative effects of cyberspace. Indeed, they need to be able to quickly address problems of digital overload and fatigue or cyberbullying and enable staff and students to engage constructively with the problematic dynamics of digital media. This is all the more important when they are engaging young people who are already experiencing, or are at risk of, mental health issues. Research on the use of digital media by young people increasingly urges balance in looking at the impacts of the internet and online technology; understanding that there are both risks and benefits to health and wellbeing; and advocating for the development of resources (in schools, community, workplaces and online) that can support young people to find their own balance in engaging with digital technology rather than dictating limits (Betton & Woollard, 2018).

SEs working in digital media therefore need to tread carefully in balancing the positive impacts of creative digital media with the potential complexities. This is particularly relevant in the context of digital storytelling, where the idea of giving young people voice can be uncritically embraced. Tania Dreher (2012), for example, argues that while much focus in youth studies is directed towards activating youth voices, there is not enough attention to the question of listening. The result, she argues, is that youth voices are being activated without being heard, particularly by those in power:

> I identify a vital challenge for the social inclusion agenda, and for participatory media: the need to not only enable the process of speaking or storytelling encapsulated in the category of 'voice', but also to ensure that the content of voice is adequately listened to. (p. 157)

Digital storytelling can certainly provide opportunities for personal expression and more empowering forms of self-representation, which can lead to more active citizenship and a democratisation of media. However, it can also lead—by virtue of being rendered a digital cultural product—to the commodification of a person's experience and, in the context of social welfare, to an even more problematic commodification of disadvantage (Gerrard, 2017). This individualisation of disadvantage, in turn, can shift an emphasis on social change away from addressing structural issues (societal inequities leading to marginalisation) to a focus on a narrative of individual suffering and resilience. As Jessica Gerrard argues in *Enterprise on the Margins*:

> Simply giving 'voice' to the marginalised and oppressed does not rectify much weightier and powerful social and economic processes of inequality within capitalism. Rather, we need—now more than ever at a time of increasing global social inequalities—accounts of inequality that squarely

face the moral, political, social, economic and cultural processes through which inequality is created, understood and made possible to intervene into. (2017, p. 4)

These complexities in how ASEs manage the risks and opportunities of digital media engagement, and the complexities of working with young people disengaged from schooling, are not well understood. Moreover, a further key research gap in this field relates to how complex forms of disengagement (economic, cultural, mental health issues) are managed and resourced in these settings. In the context of social enterprise specifically, what strategies and supports are in place to address these challenging issues while also running businesses and trying to achieve social outcomes for young people? In the next chapter, we attempt to address this question and the challenges it encapsulates, through presenting an in-depth case study of youth media organisation Youthworx, located in Melbourne, Australia. We explore the practical, lived challenges of running an art-based social enterprise that uses creative digital media to engage young people in accredited vocational training with the aim of generating pathways to further employment in the creative industries.

References

Betton, V., & Woollard, J. (2018). *Teen mental health in an online world: Supporting young people around their use of social media, apps, gaming*. Jessica Kingsley Publishers.

Borg, K., & Smith, L. (2018). Digital inclusion and online behaviour: Five typologies of Australian internet users. *Behaviour & Information Technology, 37*(4), 367–380.

Chandler, C., Dunford, M., & Bitting, S. J. (2012). *Changing young lives through media*. The Media Trust. Accessed 15 September 2021, http://www.mediatrust.org/about-media-trust/reports/

Dahlin, E. (2019). Are robots stealing our jobs? *Socius, 5*, 1–14.

Denny, S., & Seddon, F. (Eds.). (2013). *Social enterprise: Accountability and evaluation around the world*. Taylor & Francis Group.

Douglas, N. (2014). It's supposed to look like shit: The internet ugly aesthetic. *Journal of Visual Culture, 13*(3), 314–339.

Dowmunt, T., Dunford, M., & van Hemert, N. (Eds.). (2007). *Inclusion through media*. OpenMute.

Dreher, T. (2012). A partial promise of voice: Digital storytelling and the limits of listening [Paper in themed section: The media's role in social inclusion and exclusion]. *Media International Australia Incorporating Culture & Policy, 142*, 157–166.

Dunford, M., & Jenkins, T. (2018). *Digital storytelling: Form and content*. Palgrave Macmillan.

Ford, M. (2015). *Rise of the robots: Technology and the threat of a jobless future*. Basic Books.

Furlong, A. (2015). Transitions, cultures and identities: What is youth studies. In D. Woodman & A. Bennett (Eds.), *Youth cultures, transitions, and generations: Bridging the gap in youth research* (pp. 16–27). Palgrave Macmillan.

Gerrard, J. (2017). *Precarious enterprise on the margins work, poverty, and homelessness in the city* (1st ed.). Palgrave Macmillan.

Gidley, B. (2007). Beyond the numbers game: Understanding the value of participatory media. In T. Dowmunt, M. Dunford, & N. van Hemert (Eds.), *Inclusion through media* (pp. 39–61). OpenMute.

Gregory, D., Mansfield, C., & Richardson, M. (2019). *Global city challenges: The creative & social economy solution*. British Council and Social Enterprise UK. Accessed October 5 2021, https://www.socialenterprise.org.uk/international-reports/global-city-challenges-the-creative-and-social-economy-solution/

Jones, A. (2018). *Vocational education for the twenty-first century*. LH Martin Institute, University of Melbourne, Melbourne. Accessed 05 January 2022, https://melbourne-cshe.unimelb.edu.au/__data/assets/pdf_file/0011/2845775/Final-Anne-Jones-paper1.pdf

Kevelson, M. J. C., Marconi, G., Millett, C. M., & Zhelyazkova, N. (2020). *College educated yet disconnected: Exploring disconnection from education and employment in OECD countries, with a comparative focus on the U.S.* (pp. 1–29). ETS Research Report Series.

Lamb, S., Jackson, J., & Rumberger, R. (2015). *ISCY technical paper: Measuring 21st century skills in ISCY* (Technical Report). Centre for International Research on Educational Systems, Victoria University, Melbourne, VIC.

Leeuw, S. D., & Rydin, I. (2007). Migrant children's digital stories: Identity formation and self-representation through media production. *European Journal of Cultural Studies, 10*(4), 447–464.

McGregor, G., & Mills, M. (2012). Alternative education sites and marginalised young people: 'I wish there were more schools like this one'. *International Journal of Inclusive Education, 16*(8), 843–862.

Nicoli, N., Henriksen, K., Komodromos, M., & Tsagalas, D. (2021). Investigating digital storytelling for the creation of positively engaging digital content. *EuroMed Journal of Business*. Ahead of print. Accessed 21 January 2022, https://www.emerald.com/insight/content/doi/10.1108/EMJB-03-2021-0036/full/html

OECD. (2018). *Children and young people's mental health in the digital age: Shaping the future*. OECD. Accessed 21 January 2022, https://www.oecd.org/els/health-systems/Children-and-Young-People-Mental-Health-in-the-Digital-Age.pdf

O'Higgins, N. (2020). *Young people not in employment, education or training* (ILO/SIDAPartnership on Employment Technical Brief No. 3). International Labour Organisation. Accessed 15 December 2021, https://www.ilo.org/emppolicy/projects/sida/18-19/WCMS_735164/lang--en/index.htm

Poole, C. (2010). Reaching disengaged students through media skills. *Set: Research Information for Teachers* (2), 52–58.

Rennie, E., & Podkalicka, A. (2014). Youth development or media innovation? The outcomes of youth media enterprise. *Cultural Science Journal, 7*, 98–110.

Soep, E. (2006). Beyond literacy and voice in youth media production. *McGill Journal of Education, 41*(3), 197–214.

Steinkuehler, C., & King, E. (2009). Digital literacies for the disengaged: Creating after school contexts to support boys' game-based literacy skills. *On the Horizon, 17*(1), 47–59.

UNESCO. (2021, January). *The tracker: Culture and public policy*. Issue 5. Accessed 19 January 2022, https://en.unesco.org/news/tracker-culture-public-policy-issue-5

Warr, D. (2006). Gender, class, and the art and craft of social capital. *Sociological Quarterly, 47*(3), 497–520. https://doi.org/10.1111/j.1533-8525.2006.00056

3

The Youthworx Model: Disengaged Young People and Creative Digital Training

Abstract In this chapter we explore the workings of Youthworx, a creative media social enterprise in Australia that provides training, work experience and employment for young people disengaged from mainstream schooling. Drawing on the experiences of young people and staff at Youthworx, we explore three key ideas: the tension between aspirations and reality in transitioning to work in the media industries; the role of Youthworx in providing an alternative education model; and the mechanisms of creativity in digital media that can be leveraged in supporting young people experiencing barriers to mainstream education. A key concern in this chapter is to consider how the experiences and insights of Youthworx's young creatives can produce greater understanding of the benefits and challenges of bringing creative media and education together to support young people experiencing barriers to mainstream learning and employment. At the same time, while recognising the importance of enabling processes that activate young voices, we question the way 'voice' is employed in social inclusion agendas and participatory media, and insist that those voices also need to be adequately listened to and valued. We ask; in what ways can art-based social enterprises (ASEs) like

© The Author(s), under exclusive license to Springer Nature
Switzerland AG 2022
G. McQuilten et al., *Art–Based Social Enterprise, Young Creatives and the Forces of Marginalisation*, https://doi.org/10.1007/978-3-031-10925-6_3

Youthworx produce structural changes for the young people they work with?

Keywords Youthworx · Creative digital media · Social enterprise · Young creatives · Youth transitions · Participatory media · Education and training

Introduction

In this chapter, we explore the workings of Youthworx, a creative media social enterprise that provides training, work experience and employment for young people disengaged from mainstream schooling. Drawing on the experiences of young people and staff at Youthworx, we explore three key ideas: the tension between aspirations and reality in transitioning to work in the media industries; the role of Youthworx in providing an alternative education model; and the mechanisms of creativity in digital media that can be leveraged in supporting young people experiencing barriers to mainstream education. The following anecdote is about a Youthworx student, Maria, and helps set the scene for the discussion that follows:

> One of the young students we had, Maria, who had anxiety issues, whenever she held a camera, it was almost like meditation, it would sort of focus her mind on what she was seeing and what was in the square. In meditation you are sometimes asked, "What can you hear in the room? What can you see in the room? What colour is the plant?", that kind of thing. So when you're looking through a viewfinder it is similar: you're seeing the plant on the table, how is the light hitting it? Or you are listening to someone talking and they are explaining their thoughts, you are thinking about it in a different way than just being there, as you in the room. You are the filmmaker or the editor. So, whenever she had the camera, she would just be really focused and calm. (Michelle, Youthworx staff member)

This brief story of Maria speaks to the transformative potential of creative media in supporting the development of skills essential for engagement in both education and employment. In this case, Maria found the resources she needed to manage anxiety; the creative activity arrested her; and she valued having an important, circumscribed role within a professional team, which spurred her to listen, focus and engage with the learning task. Studies support this, showing that teaching media skills to young people produces pride in the collaborative production process, and by extension generates therapeutic effects and an increase in wellbeing (Gidley, 2007; Poole, 2010). Through the filming process, Maria also built confidence in her technical abilities and can be seen to be developing the possibility of seeing herself as an industry professional.

This bridge between learning skills/gaining confidence and young artists developing professional identities is a key feature of how Youthworx operates. As part of our research collaboration with Youthworx, for example, we worked with a group of emerging artists to develop new content for an exhibition. Artists Dylan Tyncherov, Dean Theilig, Cody Whelan, Will Murphy and Neithan Newton collaboratively produced a 49-minute video titled *Emerging* (2020), which weaved together interviews between the artists, and interviews with artists from one of our other case study organisations, youth performing arts company Outer Urban Projects (the focus of Chapter 7). The interviews covered a range of topics from working in the creative industries and dealing with crises to the various artists' hopes for the future. The video was installed at Bus Projects gallery (in Melbourne) over a month in early 2021.[1] In their professional and moving video work, the Youthworx artists showed both a deep engagement with the emotional and psychological complexity of living through times of crisis and also a deep pragmatism about the economic and social reality of their lives, particularly in the context of the then unfolding COVID-19 pandemic (Fig. 3.1).

As Youthworx graduate Dylan Tyncherov, who aspires to be a prolific filmmaker, described in the video:

> I think about how short fleeting life is and how anything could randomly happen. Imagine the people on the steps of Mount Vesuvius before the

---

[1] The exhibition was curated by Grace McQuilten and Amy Spiers of the research team. Bus Projects is an independent artist-run space located in the dedicated arts precinct, Collingwood Yards, in the suburb of Collingwood, Melbourne.

Fig. 3.1 Youthworx video installation, *Emerging* (2020), installed at Bus Projects, Collingwood (Photograph: Lucy Foster)

volcano erupted and they were just going about their days. A soldier's standing there and he just died. These things happen all the time – hundreds of thousands of people died – and life is fleeting and short. I am doing what I enjoy doing and there isn't too much to complain about. It's not where I'd like to be but it's a starting point to where I want to be.

A key concern in this chapter, therefore, is to consider how the experiences and insights of Youthworx creatives including Maria and Dylan can produce greater understanding of the benefits and challenges of bringing creative media and education together to support young people experiencing barriers to mainstream learning and employment. At the same time, we also consider the importance of not only enabling processes that activate young voices but, following Tanja Dreher's (2012) critique of the way 'voice' is employed in social inclusion agendas and participatory media, ensuring that those voices are also adequately listened to and valued. We ask; in what ways can art-based social enterprises (ASEs) like

Youthworx produce structural changes for the young people they work with?

A Sense of Place and a Strengths-Based Approach

The Youthworx organisation is a social enterprise and media production business that seeks to re-engage young people of 15–25 years of age who experience various forms of disengagement from education, training and employment pathways due to experiences of marginalisation. Recognising the power of creative arts to provide a sense of personal expression and efficacy, the primary means by which the Youthworx programs seek to re-engage young people is through digital media production training, along with work experience and employment in creative media production—including filmmaking, live radio broadcast and digital storytelling. Building on pre-existing skills, Youthworx expressly targets young people who have already demonstrated a flair or interest in multimedia and creativity and have existing creative hobbies such as YouTube video creation, gaming, acting, music and drawing.

Youthworx was founded by Jon Staley, a producer, writer, director and social entrepreneur who has a long-standing interest in working with young people on creative arts and media-based projects. After running some initial trials with at-risk and homeless youth at SYN Community Radio in Melbourne, Jon established Youthworx in the inner northern Melbourne suburb of Brunswick in 2008, with seed funding from the Salvation Army and ongoing support from Youth Development Australia (YDA). Brunswick is formerly a working-class neighbourhood once characterised by large communities of Italian, Greek, Turkish and Lebanese migrants and by industries such as textile manufacture and brickworks. As with major cities across the globe, the suburb is now quickly gentrifying and accommodates trendy bars and restaurants, galleries, studios and live music venues alongside second-hand opportunity shops and halal eateries. Youthworx operates out of one of Brunswick's many former industrial warehouses, situated in Tinning Street between a bustling and cosmopolitan Sydney Road and the Upfield train line. Both Youthworx's training space and a commercial arm are located in the repurposed warehouse and are furnished with industry standard, broadcast quality media equipment and resources, desktop Apple computers, soundproof recording studios and slick office furniture. This is purposeful, as Youthworx aims to provide a professional, creative studio atmosphere and dignified workplace for young people to develop skills and gain exposure to the industry of media and film production.

Youthworx's original mission was to target young people who have experienced, or are at risk of experiencing, homelessness. Over time, this remit has expanded to include a broader range of young people who encounter other barriers to conventional schooling. For many of the young people participating in Youthworx's programs, a history of disengagement is influenced by such things as neurodiversity, anxiety, depression, psychosocial disability and other struggles with mental health and wellbeing, all resulting in learning disruptions and difficulties. Other factors affecting engagement for some students include new migrant or refugee status, as well as a lack of family support and unstable housing. Studies show that young people struggling with these kinds of barriers to learning have lower educational and employment outcomes, with disengagement from education leading to serious consequences for their futures (McGregor & Mills, 2012; Orygen, 2014). Similarly, studies demonstrate that concerted engagement and early intervention programs aimed at supporting disadvantaged students to obtain secondary and further education, such as Youthworx's programs, are vital to improving work prospects into the future (Orygen, 2014; Waghorn et al., 2012).

The key principles of the Youthworx model are underpinned by a strengths-based approach. On their website, they claim that their aim is to provide 'an environment conducive to bringing out the best in people by drawing on their creativity and giving them the tools to be articulate in their experience of the world' (Youthworx, 2021). This is achieved via small class sizes of 12–15 students and a unique collaborative studio classroom model and multilayered staffing structure that, in addition to the class teacher, also includes a youth worker, a job pathways coordinator and media industry professional in order to provide additional guidance and support to students (Youthworx, 2021). The intention is to offer an alternative model to conventional training courses that facilitates the best possible chance for struggling students to succeed. As Jon has explained:

> The reason that we have the extra support – the reason that we have a youth worker and an industry person inside the program – is so it's not just another TAFE (Technical and Further Education) course, so it does cater for kids who are at risk.

Youthworx is thus designed to be a creative and engaging alternative to traditional education and employment initiatives, operating as both a generative creative studio and supportive community space. This was evident when Jon described the spaces at Youthworx:

> I had observed in some youth spaces that young people were tagging all over the tables and all over the computers. I didn't want that. I wanted this to be an environment where they got the opportunity to be creative, be productive and produce the highest possible level content that they could. We wanted to create a quality experience for young people, something that was a bit different to a traditional classroom or a youth hangout space.

This strengths-based approach to learning—in line with similar educational settings—builds on the notion that young people from less privileged or advantaged backgrounds can be empowered to become successful in their own right, rather than by virtue of being 'helped' (Lee et al., 2020; Rennie & Podkalicka, 2014). As Jon pointed out, 'You've got to start off with "What can they be", rather than, "what aren't they?"'.

Youthworx therefore aims to provide a safe, dignified and professionalised space for young people to gain life skills, re-engage with the world and unlock their creative potential in ways that will serve them into the future, regardless of whether they choose to have an ongoing career in media production or the creative industries. Jon described the training program as an alternative education and reengagement program, where students can explore existing creative passions, discover new ones and 'realise something about themselves'. He further explained:

I want participants to experience producing at a high level because when you start to see what you can create at this level, you start to place value on your work. And then by extension, you start to place value on yourself. And when you place value on yourself, you're more motivated to go to the next step. And when you're more motivated to go to the next step, you're more motivated to deal with the other issues in your life.

Employment in Digital Media: Aspiration Versus Reality

The majority of Youthworx students we interviewed aspire to work in creative media production, with many students expressing a desire to go on to do further study in a range of roles including video editing, game design, 3D model building, camera operation, acting or script writing. A number of students thus have high aspirations of working in the film industry in some capacity. Emir, for example, lit up when talking of his hopes to do visual effects and editing for Marvel studios or, as a 'Plan B', prop and costume making. Emir explained that training at Youthworx has made these dreams feel more obtainable: 'It's more like a dream that I didn't think would come true that has come true'.

Other students, however, are more pragmatic about their prospects and realise they face multiple barriers to pursuing a career in media production. These barriers include the lack of representation of women in the media industry, reflected in recent Youthworx classes, where out of a cohort of 15 only two are female. Other barriers are financial. Some students, such as Liam, noted that certain media jobs don't represent a 'good future', are costly to get training in and promise little return on investment. Similarly, Anthony was equally cautious about the prospect of pursuing a creative career in music, insisting that it can't be his main occupation because it won't make him a lot of money. Additionally, Youthworx staff themselves also express doubts that what they are doing produces reliable employment outcomes for the young people they train. Grant, for example, was aware that Youthworx programs are celebrated because they offer storytelling and creative digital skills to young people impacted by marginalisation, but wonders 'does it get you a job?'. Grant expressed concern about the employment prospects of students: 'they'll probably never be able to work in this industry because the industry itself is so competitive and they're starting way behind'.

This issue of barriers to mainstream employment in the creative industries is a consistent theme across the various case studies in this book. Despite the potential job readiness of the young people trained through arts-based social enterprises such as Youthworx, structural barriers remain ever-present. The highly competitive media and arts industry remains one that has little capacity to accommodate young aspiring digital content producers with complex backgrounds and needs, nor much incentive to do so. In this context, organisations such as Youthworx are advocating for the industry to be more socially inclusive of young people impacted by forces of marginalisation. As staff member Diane put it:

> There's also two parts to it: you can send people out who are robust and ready for the mainstream; or you can communicate with the partners that they should step up, and take on people that might not quite be there yet.

One way Youthworx tries to combat the structural inequalities of the media industry and encourage inclusive hiring practices is to generate work experience and employment within the business arm of Youthworx Productions—and to increase their commercial operations to create more employment opportunities and pathways to industry. Staff, however, are aware these opportunities are limited—with often just one or two trainee places offered per year, while the work available varies due to the fluctuations of short-term contract work. This inconsistency is felt by Youthworx students who aspire to work for the business. Liam noted:

> I have a really conflicting thing for next year. I don't know whether to further my study in this area of study or get a job next door. I was hoping to work next door, but […] I don't know whether it would only be a short term sort of thing. […] I don't want to start working here and then, six months down the road, they go, we have to give you less shifts or something like that.

Understanding the realities of the business, while somewhat confronting, does give students valuable insights into how the media industry operates. Real industry experience is a feature of the learning experience for students. In turn, this instils confidence and emboldens them to produce their own work. The training and work experience provided by Youthworx also broaden graduates' skills-base to include entrepreneurial and other twenty-first-century skills and competencies, as discussed in Chapter 2, which can equip students with a resourcefulness to navigate the gigging economy of the creative industries and initiate their own income-generating projects (Lamb et al., 2015; World Economic Forum, 2016). Some tenacious and committed former students, for example, described being supported by Youthworx after graduating with after-hours access to editing facilities and camera gear, or assistance with funding applications for short film and media projects. As Idris explained after discovering it was difficult to obtain work in the film industry: 'that's when I said "you know what, if they're not going to give me a job, I'll make my own job"'.

An Alternative Education and Reengagement Space, Before a Media School

While direct employment transitions into the creative media industry may not always be a realistic outcome for students at Youthworx, the alternative education model employed by the organisation provides crucial building blocks to develop skills, confidence and capacity to transition into further work and study. While government and funders frequently require social enterprises to provide evidence and reporting of impact, this is often narrowly understood with regard to transitioning young people into study or work. One of the main outcomes reported for young people participating in Youthworx's programs, above and beyond employment or educational attainment, was improved health and wellbeing. This included an increased sense of support and community, confidence in learning, connection to the creative industries, and developing hope and resilience for their future. Engagement and wellbeing, as we argue, are crucial precursors to generating positive pathways for young people experiencing barriers to education, and they underpin the development of skills and transitions to further employment or education (Kelly et al., 2019).

These findings are supported by observations by Youthworx staff who report the primary goal and success of the program are that it re-engages disengaged and vulnerable young people. Diane, for example, noted, 'This is primarily an alternative education space, to help people build their confidence and resilience, before it's a media school'. Wellbeing is identified by staff as being crucial in helping young people re-engage and transition to further study and work. Grant explained:

> I mean, if you want to improve someone's ability to engage and listen and be motivated, wellbeing is crucial […] How are you going to learn anything if you're just hungry and tired and mentally juggling whatever?

In terms of wellbeing, having a place to come to and simply being involved is understood by staff as offering a support network, sense of purpose and a place to feel welcome or that helps them feel more resilient and connected. As Grant further observed:

> That's what keeps everyone going, is knowing that you are providing a safe place for these kids to come to and actually seeing the changes in people. Like Samuel, for example, he is intensely shy and quiet and came in here barely saying a word and it turns out his uncle is a filmmaker and he had this passion inside him and by the end of the term he was acting in films and editing, he became one of our best editors in the class and he is only 16-17.

Students also speak to the importance and potential outcomes of this sense of inclusion and belonging. Idris, for example, described: 'they've given me a welcoming space, a welcoming presence. I like to be here, because it influences me and it inspires me to create'.

Given the contradictions and tensions that come with the aspiration to pursue further education and employment, staff acknowledge that the key transition most young people experience through the Youthworx program is an increased motivation for 'further study and growth'.

This openness to explore further education is a major step and significant change for many Youthworx students. As Grant observed, 'we're working on the coal face here with kids who, the backgrounds they've come from, they probably have never even thought about going to uni'. As other research into youth engagement through digital media has identified, one of the 'soft life skills' participatory media training can offer young people is *learning to learn* (Chandler et al., 2012; Gidley, 2007, p. 54). This is certainly the case for Youthworx cohorts. Staff member Michelle explained:

> So, students who haven't even finished up to year seven and then they come to us, they never thought they would be able to do it, they come out with certificate II and then continue in certificate III and then they might go and do another TAFE course after that. There is a huge leap from when they first started and they don't even know what they are doing there, they are just a bit nervous that they are there and they have some sort of imposter syndrome or something.

Creativity Builds Confidence: 'The Subject Is the Hook'

The creative focus of Youthworx's programs in digital media offers an important lever for engaging their students. Learning skills in video production, for example, activates existing interests, knowledge and in some cases passions of students. As Grant described:

> They're already connected to media; 90% of them are absolutely saturated by their gaming and all their devices, they're part of the media landscape. You can activate people's creativity and passion through that.

As outlined in Chapter 2, existing research points clearly to this strong connection between young people, creativity and media engagement. Walsh et al. (2011) report, for example, that 'Information Communication Technology is a way of life for most Australian young people. It is central to the way in which they learn, relate and make meaning in their everyday lives' (p. 14). This pre-existing interest in media acts as a 'hook' for engagement in the Youthworx program, in the way that the arts or sport has been observed as acting as a 'hook' in other at-risk youth engagement projects (Gidley, 2007, p. 42). As staff member Polly reported:

> The subject is the hook that is getting them in here on time three days a week [...] we have students that travel from [outer Melbourne suburbs] Sunbury, Werribee, all over. Some of them will travel an hour-and-a-half to get here on public transport. So there's a fair bit of commitment there.

This style of interest-driven learning using digital media has been shown to have significant positive results for disengaged youth, including those impacted by forces of marginalisation, with other studies similarly finding that disengaged students are motivated to travel long distances to attend alternative schools with flexible learning environments that address their diverse and complex needs (Ito et al., 2010; McGregor & Mills, 2012; Vickery, 2017). In their study of how young people engage with new media, *Hanging Out, Messing Around, and Geeking Out* (2010), for example, Mizuko Ito and her team identified a group of young people who participated in digital media culture and creation through 'interest-driven practices', finding that their existing passions in 'certain specialised activities, interests, or niche and marginalised identities' drove them to engage with new media to find like-minded networks and online communities (p. 16). The young people who engage in interest-driven practices reflect the Youthworx cohort we interviewed and are 'kids who are identified as smart, different, or creative, who generally exist at the margins of teen social worlds' (Ito et al., 2010, p. 16). Such young people have developed hobbies or career interests that might not be represented in their local communities and aren't supported through conventional schooling, and as such 'require more far-flung networks of affiliation and expertise' (Ito et al., 2010, p. 16).

Young people at Youthworx are therefore motivated to attend classes, in different ways to mainstream schooling, as they are studying a subject that engages them creatively and activates their passions. Students we interviewed support this notion, noting that they were flourishing at

Youthworx with access to training and resources that furthered their passions. As Anthony reflected:

> I've been able to talk to people and meet some people I enjoy and then relate to them. Because sometimes you, I think, subconsciously you feel alone when you don't see anyone else that's going through the same things – maybe because you're boxed in on Instagram. But there's been people that have been through similar stuff to me, so then I can find solace in that.

This connection to new networks of friends and supports is a significant part of the Youthworx model, which, as described above, includes older mentors and industry professionals as well as younger peers who share and encourage their interests. As discussed in Chapter 2, these 'bridging networks' are important for developing social capital and opportunities for work beyond a young person's immediate contacts.

In addition to being surrounded by people who support and understand their struggles and pursuits, Youthworx provides flexible schedules and support not typically offered in mainstream schooling. For example, Emir noted that Youthworx had offered him flexibility, understanding and the 'courtesy' to leave early or take time out that he hadn't experienced in his old school. This had left him feeling like he was fitting-in and consequently managing the pressures of study better:

> Like, I'm in my own environment. Let's say a fish has to be in water. I'm probably the fish that's in the water now. Because before, it's like I'm somewhere that I can't – a fish can't breathe out of water, so I couldn't really cope with that school, but I can cope where I am now.

A further, and more specific, finding from our interviews is that media practices have particular benefit for some young people who struggle with anxiety and other psychosocial conditions. As evident in the story of Maria that began this chapter, Youthworx staff report that the nature of using the camera equipment, recording devices and editing software helps to act as a mediator or buffer between the young creative and the world, and many participants in the Youthworx program find it easier to express themselves using technology. This finding is supported by studies that have found that the filmmaking process is therapeutic to young people struggling with autism spectrum disorder, mental ill-health or anxiety and has a significant impact on autonomy, awareness and self-confidence (Chandler et al., 2012; Poole, 2010; Saladino et al., 2020).

Staff member Michelle noted that digital tools, particularly cameras, provide young people with 'an ability to express themselves and get beyond themselves and get out of their heads […] it is a tool to take the anxiety away'. Michelle continued:

> People who have trouble with 'voice', expressing themselves or even talking to one person, let alone a group of people, can find a different way to do it by piecing together interviews or showing something to their class and the class responding to that; it is a different kind of dialogue. […] The actual creating side of it does give them a different way to speak and communicate. For someone who has anxiety, for instance, just to walk into a space like this and stand there, they can be quite nervous. If you walk into a space and you are holding a camera or a microphone, however, you have got a job. It gives you a purpose and a buffer.

Students also relish the focused, consuming nature of media work. This became clear when Youthworx graduate Idris talked about editing:

> I enjoyed editing because there's something about it that just puts me in flow and I just completely forget about the outside world; I'm sort of focused on seeing the end result. I already see it, and I'm going after it to make it as perfect as it can be.

It has been noted in related research that recognising and overcoming challenges thrown up by the media production process and the transformative moment at which a professional role is taken on can be enormously empowering for young people (Gidley, 2007, p. 49). It has also been noted that participating in and creating digital and online media can facilitate a distraction and escapism from distressing emotions for young people, and that balancing passive media consumption with the active creation of media content can enable young people to develop their self-worth and self-efficacy (Betton & Woollard, 2018). This was evident, for example, when Youthworx student Gavin observed changes to his mood after studying at Youthworx: 'At present, I'm generally a lot happier. There are definitely many times when it drops but it's better. I'm feeling occupied so when I'm in class I can't think about bad shit and then start to spiral'.

No Ordinary Classroom: Professional Experiences in the Media Industry

Jon has described Youthworx's program as aimed at a model of delivery that is 'very much around a collaborative, kind of creative studio style of teaching and learning as opposed to a classroom style' where the aim is for hands-on, practical learning in a professional media industry environment. The professional, creative studio model for learning was evident in the Youthworx students' collaborative video work, *Emerging*. As introduced at the start of the chapter, this work by Dylan Tyncherov, Dean Theilig, Cody Whelan, Will Murphy and Neithan Newton was presented as a dual channel video installation at Bus Galleries. One video presented formal headshot interviews with a Youthworx or Outer Urban Projects student, while an adjacent video presented behind-the-scenes 'making-of' footage showing the production team. It demonstrated the professional, teamwork-oriented learning environment where everyone has a role in the production, with one student holding a boom mic, another listening in with headphones, while others positioned lighting and operated cameras. This was no ordinary classroom (Figs. 3.2 and 3.3).

Youthworx student Gavin echoed this sentiment when he noted 'I think sitting in class listening to teachers explain stuff, it's not as effective for me as a learner because I'm definitely hands-on and I learn by doing'. Anthony also described:

> Some days are boring because we might just be listening and listening [...] that's the stuff that I can't focus on. That's when I do dumb stuff that will get me in trouble. But if we have a good mix of practicality and then watching something, visual learning and writing a little bit – that's

Fig. 3.2 Youthworx video installation, *Emerging* (2020), installed at Bus Projects, Collingwood (Photograph: Lucy Foster)

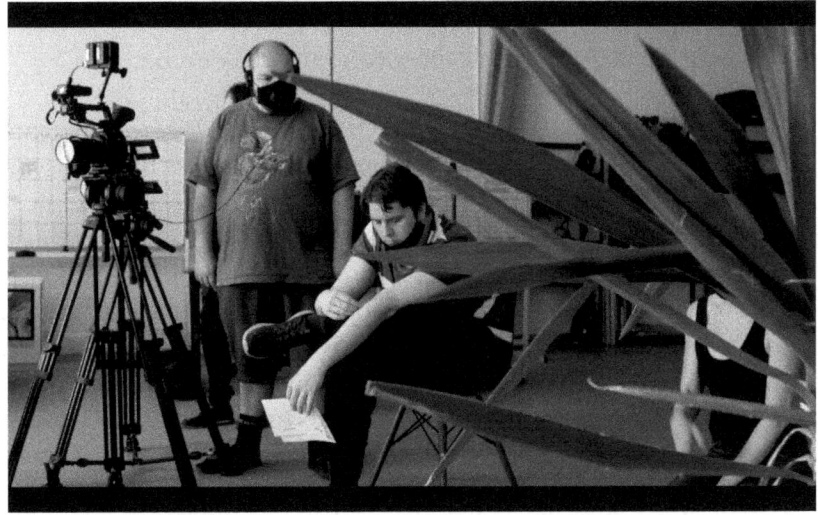

Fig. 3.3 A 'making-of' scene from *Emerging* (2020) (Image courtesy of the artists and Youthworx)

really good for me. And we do more of that than anywhere else education wise [...] I haven't missed a day [...] I think I'm the only one who's had perfect attendance.

These observations accord with related research on the educational possibilities of the creative media space. The Beyond the Numbers Game research project at Goldsmiths, University of London, for example, examined a number of case studies in inclusive media, noting that the 'professionalism' of having a specific formal role in a production team is beneficial for young people (Gidley, 2007, p. 48). Indeed, these researchers observed that young people flourish in the intensity and collaborative nature of the media production process, which provides 'buzz', 'glamour and kudos', while building confidence in what an individual can contribute while working in a team and relying on others (Gidley, 2007, p. 47). Ben Gidley (2007) observed that a key aspect of this was the collaborative dimension:

> Different participants' individual creativity makes a significant difference to the endeavour. In the production crew, each individual participant brings unique qualities and thus makes a unique difference – their presence is not interchangeable with that of any other person. (p. 47)

In this way, collaboration in participatory media has the potential to allow young people impacted by marginalisation to move beyond their individual experiences—and towards shared or collective forms of identity construction.

Youthworx participants are also supported to develop industry networks which extend to the development of professional, public outcomes of their creative outputs including broadcasting and distributing their work on community radio and television (SYN radio and Channel 31), through public screenings and film festivals, as well as online. In our experience with the screening of the video produced by Youthworx artists at Bus Projects, it was not simply the screening of their work in the gallery that mattered. Importantly, the artists had an opportunity to present their work to a range of audiences including their friends and family, as well as professional visual arts and youth arts audiences. This was facilitated through an exhibition opening for the general public and a public program that included a Q&A session with the Youthworx artists. The Q&A session, in particular, allowed the artists to present their work as emerging professionals and explain their motivations and creative aims. Finding diverse audiences for the work of Youthworx artists meant that there was a greater opportunity for their voices not only to be activated, but also to be heard (Dreher, 2012).

Adapting Mission to Young People's Needs

A further notable aspect of the Youthworx approach, and an issue with which we bring this chapter to an end, relates to cohort history and transition. Michelle described earlier cohorts as being 'tough and rough' with various presenting challenges such as substance abuse issues and unstable housing. Increasingly, however, the program is attracting young people who are from more economically stable families but are, as Michelle put it, 'anxious, addicted to their phones and on the spectrum'. This change in cohort is attributed to a change in outreach and referral processes. As Polly observed:

> When I first started here, there were a lot more young people coming directly from youth hostels and places like that. I know that the previous youth worker was able to go out and visit those hostels. We can't do that now because they all run through the central system, so it's very difficult to even get an address for a youth hostel to go and knock on the door and say, "Hey, have you got any young people that might want to come along to the program?"...I think too, over the years, the compliance in terms of the qualifications has increased. A lot of the young people that used to suit this course, [had] really chaotic lifestyles, and just couldn't cope with the attendance requirements and that's what's actually needed now. We're finding that we're probably sourcing more of our young people straight from schools. We've got wellbeing coordinators phoning and saying, "Look, we've got this young boy in year ten. He's not attending. He wants to be a YouTuber," which is what most of the young people say when they come along. They all want to make films for YouTube. So yes, more students are being referred that way.

This shift in cohort and adaptation of mission is significant and points to the challenges that social enterprises face in bringing together complex and competing goals—in this case, a formally recognised vocational training program that provides significant benefits in terms of skills and industry pathways, and yet may not fit the needs of emerging cohorts of young participants, particularly those disengaged from schooling. Accredited training offers the benefits of recognition of skills, and more concrete transitions into further study and work; however, the more collaborative and creative nature of media production isn't easily translated into the formal structures of accreditation. This, in turn, can dis-incentivise participation for those with learning needs, language barriers or who struggle with the limitation of formal study. Ben Gidley (2007) discusses these complexities in relation to participatory media and communities experiencing forms of marginalisation:

> The intensity, the non-linear un-folding and the collaborative nature of media might, therefore, fit better with the relatively informal pedagogical models which have been more typical of participatory media. Consequently, a shift to an accreditation model needs to be managed very carefully. (pp. 53–54)

In the case of Youthworx, then, their mission has evolved in response to what has been possible in terms of the delivery of training, which has meant focusing more deliberately on young people with mental health issues, learning difficulties and disengagement from schooling, rather than those directly experiencing homelessness and more entrenched forms of poverty. This shift is nevertheless understood by staff as a positive one. As Polly commented, 'the right students are here' and 'everyone that's in the program has reason to be here'. Joanna supported this observation:

> We have moved away a little bit from the pointy end [of homelessness] but, actually, when you look more into that, they [the program participants] very much do fit at risk of homelessness criteria [...] So if you have a learning disability, and do not have much family support, and do not know how to navigate the world that well, you are definitely at risk of homelessness.

A further notable facet of these changing cohorts concerns gender. As mentioned earlier in relation to job transitions into the media industry, there are very few female students at Youthworx. Staff attribute this to the referral processes that are in place to connect young people to the programs that Youthworx provides. As one staff member, Joanne, observed in one of our interviews, 'the youth refuges, it was always males that were referred in'. In addition, there was a suggestion that gender norms and societal expectations in relation to creative practices common in digital media made for difficulty in engaging young women in Youthworx programs. As Joanne observed, 'it feels like media is still male dominated'. In the light of this, new outreach and promotional initiatives to expressly target young female aspiring filmmakers were developed in 2019 (Youthworx, 2019).

Conclusion

The experiences of students and staff at Youthworx highlight a number of issues both specific to Youthworx and common to ASEs. These issues include the simultaneous push–pull of the creative industries for employment pathways for young people experiencing barriers to education and work; the ways in which ASEs challenge mainstream industry to be more inclusive of people impacted by the forces of marginalisation; tensions in the ways vocational training programs formalise creative education and in so doing, can impact negatively on qualities of engagement and access; and the positive wellbeing impacts of simply being involved in creative learning, which exceed and run counter to the more utilitarian impulses of achieving educational and work outcomes or 'transitions'.

With these issues in mind, the Youthworx approach to learning for young people disengaged from school and work testifies to the importance and benefits of facilitating wellbeing through creative training practices. To return to the question that started the discussion in this chapter, what structural changes are ASEs like Youthworx able to produce for their young artists? As we have demonstrated, Youthworx challenges the norms of media industries and highlights the important ways in which creative media help young people navigate, express and share their emotional and psychological experiences of the world. Not only does Youthworx provide avenues for young people to have a voice and express their understanding of the world, but through the development of professional practices and access to industry opportunities and experience, they build the foundations for these voices to be heard. Further, they offer practical alternatives to mainstream education and employment that, in turn, demonstrate to industry and educational providers the possibility and benefits of alternative structures and approaches to inclusivity. Finally, Youthworx creates a space that young people want to come to, develop their creativity and participate in, and which activates their hopes for the future. This sense of engagement and belonging is an essential precursor to engaging in further education and work, despite the systemic barriers to training and employment faced by many young people, especially those impacted by forces of marginalisation.

References

Betton, V., & Woollard, J. (2018). *Teen mental health in an online world: Supporting young people around their use of social media, apps, gaming*. Jessica Kingsley Publishers.

Chandler, C., Dunford, M., & Bitting, S. J. (2012). *Changing young lives through media*. The Media Trust. Accessed 15 September 2021, http://www.mediatrust.org/about-media-trust/reports/

Dreher, T. (2012). A partial promise of voice: Digital storytelling and the limits of listening [Paper in themed section: The media's role in social inclusion and exclusion]. *Media International Australia Incorporating Culture & Policy, 142*, 157–166.

Gidley, B. (2007). Beyond the numbers game: Understanding the value of participatory media. In T. Dowmunt, M. Dunford, & N. van Hemert (Eds.), *Inclusion through media* (pp. 39–61). OpenMute.

Ito, M., Baumer, S., Bittanti, M., Boyd, D., Cody, R., Herr-Stephenson, B., Horst, H. A., Lange, P. G., Mahendran, D., Martìnez, K. Z., & Pascoe, C. J. (2010). *Hanging out, messing around, and geeking out: Kids living and learning with new media*. MIT Press.

Kelly, P., Campbell, P., & Howie, L. (2019). *Rethinking young people's marginalisation: Beyond neo-liberal futures?* Routledge.

Lamb, S., Jackson, J., & Rumberger, R. (2015). *ISCY technical paper: Measuring 21st century skills in ISCY*. Centre for International Research on Education Systems, Victoria University. Accessed 30 September 2020, http://vuir.vu.edu.au/31682/1/ISCY%2021st%20Century%20Skills%20Framework.pdf

Lee, E., Black, M., Falkmer, M., et al. (2020). "We can see a bright future": Parents' perceptions of the outcomes of participating in a strengths-based program for adolescents with autism spectrum disorder. *Journal of Autism & Development Disorders, 50*, 3179–3194.

McGregor, G., & Mills, M. (2012). Alternative education sites and marginalised young people: "I wish there were more schools like this one". *International Journal of Inclusive Education, 16*(8), 843–862.

Orygen Youth Health Research Centre. (2014). *Tell them they're dreaming: Work, education and young people with mental illness in Australia*. Orygen Youth Health Research Centre, Melbourne.

Poole, C. (2010). Reaching disengaged students through media skills. *Set: Research Information for Teachers* (2), 52–58.

Rennie, E., & Podkalicka, A. (2014). Youth development or media innovation? The outcomes of youth media enterprise. *Cultural Science Journal, 7*, 98–110.

Saladino, V., Sabatino, A., Iannaccone, C., Pastorino, G., & Verrastro, V. (2020). Filmmaking and video as therapeutic tools: Case studies on autism spectrum disorder. *The Arts in Psychotherapy, 71*, 1–16.

Vickery, J. R. (2017). *Worried about the wrong things: Youth, risk, and opportunity in the digital world*. MIT Press.

Waghorn, G., Sukanta, S., Harvey, C., Morgan, V., et al. (2012). "Earning and learning" in those with psychotic disorders: The second Australian national survey of psychosis. *Australian & New Zealand Journal of Psychiatry, 46*(8), 774–785.

Walsh, L., Lemon, B., Black, R., Mangan, C., & Collin, P. (2011). *The role of technology in engaging disengaged youth*. The Australian Flexible Learning Framework, Canberra.

World Economic Forum. (2016). *New vision for education: Fostering social and emotional learning through technology*. World Economic Forum. Accessed 30 September 2020, http://www3.weforum.org/docs/WEF_New_Vision_for_Education.pdf

Youthworx. (2019, May). *Girls! Believe in yourselves*. Youthworx YouTube Channel. Accessed 20 January 2022, https://youtu.be/Ega1Zuske6A

Youthworx. (2021). *Our impact*. Youthworx Website. Accessed 21 April 2021, https://youthworxproductions.com.au/our-impact

4

Fashioning a Future: Material Practice, Creativity and Sustainable Economies

Abstract Creative material practice, in both differing and similar ways to technological and digital creative processes, has the ability to engage young people who face barriers to mainstream education but who may lack digital literacy skills. This chapter will thus look at art-based social enterprises that engage with textiles and fashion with the specific aim of addressing barriers to employment for young creatives affected by the impacts of migration and displacement. How are craft and textile forms leveraged for learning models that engage young people who have had disengaged prior experiences of education or lacked prior schooling due to the dislocating effects of the migration experience? In the specific context of migration and displacement, material practice draws on cultural traditions and existing creative skills. These skills and aesthetic forms can be deliberately re-oriented to new marketplaces through contemporary fashion, craft and textile design, which in turn support young people to position themselves as creative actors in contemporary global culture/s. This potential is evident in examples of fashion and craft-based social enterprise across both developing and developed economies, and aligns with UNESCO's advocacy for creative practice that builds on and sustains cultural practice. Yet with the realities of limited funding and the precarious market for fashion retail globally, how ambitious can fashion and craft based ASEs be in imagining their development and growth in terms of the scope and impact of the training programs they offer?

Keywords Young creatives · Migration · Craft · Fashion and textiles · Material practice · Social enterprise · Employment · Education and training

Introduction

Creative material practice, in both differing and similar ways to technological and digital creative processes, has the ability to engage young people who face barriers to mainstream education but who may lack digital literacy skills. This chapter will thus look at ASEs that engage not with the digital, but with textiles and fashion, and with the specific aim of addressing barriers to employment for young creatives affected by the impacts of migration and displacement. How are craft and textile forms leveraged for learning models that engage young people who have had disengaged prior experiences of education or lacked prior schooling due to the dislocating effects of the migration experience? In the specific context of migration and displacement, material practice draws on cultural traditions and existing creative skills. These skills and aesthetic forms can be deliberately re-oriented to new marketplaces through contemporary fashion, craft and textile design, which in turn support young people to position themselves as creative actors in contemporary global culture/s. This potential is evident in examples of fashion and craft-based social enterprise across both developing and developed economies, and aligns with UNESCO's advocacy for creative practice that builds on and sustains cultural practice (UNESCO, 2013). Yet with the realities of limited funding and the precarious market for fashion retail globally, how ambitious can fashion and craft-based ASEs be in imagining their development and growth in terms of the scope and impact of the training programs they offer?

In *Be Creative* (2016), Angela McRobbie makes a compelling case for fashion-based social or micro-enterprise to provide a vehicle for meaningful (if not lucrative) work for young creatives wrestling with the exigencies of a neoliberal world. McRobbie brings a feminist perspective to this issue and challenges some of the inherent assumptions characteristic of a capitalist economy; perhaps most significantly that 'making money' is the primary driver of how we orient to work. McRobbie focuses primarily on women in fashion enterprises in Berlin and compares this context to the conditions of the fashion economy in the UK. She takes into account the move towards ethical and sustainable fashion and discusses examples of fashion enterprises that also have a social purpose, for example in providing employment in production and manufacturing to migrant women. Nevertheless, the focus of *Be Creative* is expressly on the experience of young creatives from the 'middle classes' (p. 189) and so the specific conditions experienced by migrant women, or migrant communities, are somewhat peripheral to what is a nuanced and complex discussion of creative work as a radical practice in twenty-first-century workscapes.

In fact, this class differential is common to much of the literature on fashion-based social enterprise, in which migrant workers, both local and global, are envisaged as the 'beneficiaries' of (predominantly) production work available in the more industrial terrain of the fashion industry. This thematic in the literature speaks, in fact, to structural inequities in the very make-up of the design and fashion creative industries, where the role of designer is geared towards highly educated and more networked creative individuals (somewhat but not always distinct from the processes of production), while the role of producer is more accessible to people with less education and social capital.

Expanding beyond this Eurocentric view of fashion-based social enterprise, however, brings other perspectives, including one that grasps the agency of diverse cultural and ethnic groups in design and entrepreneurship, and reciprocally, the potential of fashion-based enterprise to support economic, educational and social development for migrant and ethnic communities. This chapter will explore some of these tensions and complexities in understanding the possibilities of fashion and art-based social enterprises in contributing to sustainable cultural, economic and social development for young people from migrant and refugee backgrounds. These possibilities are balanced against the extremely challenging context of global fashion markets, which are increasingly coalescing around large-scale 'mega-brands' and fast fashion, with potentially devastating environmental and social consequences. As Alice Payne writes in *Designing Fashion's Future* (2021):

> Although the critiques of fast fashion hold true for many other fashion systems, in the fast fashion of multinational retailers, the problems reach their apogee. All issues are exacerbated: the waste, the reliance on fossil fuels, the opaque supply chains, the need for perpetual growth to satisfy shareholders, the environmental and social damage externalized. (p. 97)

Creative Economy and Social Enterprise

As discussed in Chapter 1, in 2021, the United Nations passed a resolution declaring it the International Year of Creative Economy for Sustainable Development—in both recognition of the capacity for culture and creativity to support more sustainable forms of development, but also to provide much needed critical support and advocacy for the cultural and creative industries in crisis due to the impacts of the COVID-19 pandemic (UNESCO, 2021). UNESCO, as the UN's cultural agency, has therefore sharpened their focus on this dual advocacy. The potential of creativity and culture to support the advancement of communities impacted by marginalisation was manifest in a UNESCO 'Roadmap' report that expanded on the UN resolution:

> Today, creativity is increasingly recognized as a renewable, omnipresent resource for sustainable, human-centric development. A creative economy founded upon respect for freedom of expression and cultural rights can also galvanise inclusive, tolerant and peaceful societies. It can also empower and engage various vulnerable and at times marginalized groups within societies. (p. 1)

This builds on the 2013 UNESCO Creative Economy Report which emphasised the ways in which creativity can support the economic and social development of communities by harnessing existing skills and cultural knowledge to increase income generation while preserving culture—moving away from the more extractive impacts of global development and the imposition of industries that create negative environmental and social impacts (UNESCO, 2013).

These arguments lend significant support to the combined social and economic value of craft and textile practices, which augment a growing body of literature addressing the social benefits of 'making together' in relation to textiles, craft and fibre art practices. Participatory textile practices are understood to facilitate communication, cultural exchange, building community and fostering social bonds (Gibson, 2016; Shercliff, 2015; Shercliff & Twigger Holroyd, 2016). As Robertson and Vinebaum (2016) write:

> Whether bringing people together in physical or digital spaces or both, artists are mobilizing textiles to spur interpersonal dialog and exchange, and to educate, build community, and advocate for social change. Their projects create social bonds and foster new types of community, some fleeting and temporary, and others more long term and durational. (p. 3)

Parallel to these interests in the social benefits of craft and textile practices is an equally relevant trajectory in craft activism, or 'craftivism', that draws on feminist critiques of the conditions of domestic labour and understandings of social hierarchies of value (Greer, 2014). Historically, craft and textile practices have been undervalued in numerous ways: for example, being of cultural or societal value, of value in the art world and of value in economic or market terms (Robertson & Vinebaum, 2016). In the context of the creative practices of ethnic minority and Indigenous communities, there is a similar tension in how traditional fibre-based cultural practices are understood and received in contemporary art value chains (Haraway, 2016). Craftivism therefore reclaims the social and political value of craft practices in works that bring craft, from knitting and weaving to embroidery and beading, into public spaces, often with a social justice imperative.

The term 'craftivism' was coined by the writer Besty Greer in 2003, referring to practices that combine domestic craft, such as yarning, knitting and cross-stitch, with social justice and community activism. Yarnbombing, where public spaces are occupied and reclaimed through colourful and decorative wool-based decoration, is probably the most well-known iteration of craftivist tactics. While craft practices have been used strategically in a range of feminist art practices, with particular emphasis in the second wave of feminism in the 1960s, more recent forms of craftivism have tended to encompass a range of left-wing and social justice causes including environmentalism, anti-capitalism and anti-war movements. In the work *Pink Tank* (2006), for example, Danish artist Marianne Jørgensen figuratively hijacked a World War II combat tank as a protest against the Danish and Western involvement in the then war in Iraq. The tank, a masculine symbol of military strength and power, was effectively emasculated, covered instead with pink crochet and knitted squares. Political groups such as the *Knitting Nannas Against Gas* (KNAG) collective, established in New South Wales (Australia), also have a direct protest mission—in this instance to stop gas mining in agricultural land. For KNAG, knitting is a tool for non-violent political activism:

> KNAG use non-violent direct action, with a spin suiting the capabilities of older women. 'Sit, knit, plot' describes the formula for protest knit-ins at locations where they can be visible, talking with passers-by about the effects of fracking and fossil fuels on individuals, communities and environments. (KNAG, 2021)

Craftivist practices also subvert conventional ideas of functionality, utility and commercial value—and this is a common theme in the literature on participatory textile practices, which tend to be less market-oriented. Partly as a consequence of this focus on the social (and potentially radical) dimension of craft and textile practices, the underlying issue of how these practices are valued (or undervalued) in markets remains live (Hughes, 2012). Meanwhile, migrant and refugee communities have less visibility in craftivist discourses, perhaps because these practices tend towards Western feminist perspectives, and also because more direct forms of activism can be highly risky for individuals who have short-term or precarious visa status, where any kind of interaction with the policing or justice system can impact on attaining permanent residency (Kocher & Stuesse, 2021; McQuilten, 2019). Perhaps most significantly, migrant communities have a greater imperative to direct craft and textile practices towards income generation (Bhachu, 2021).

Social enterprise therefore offers an interesting possibility of bringing together the social justice values and history of textile and craft practices with more directly focused market activity to support this income generation, especially for communities impacted by marginalisation (McQuilten, 2017; McQuilten & White, 2016). While this may seem 'instrumentalist' from the vantage point of art discourses (Dickens & Lonie, 2013), it speaks to the limitations of these discourses in understanding the experiences and needs of creative communities facing forms of marginalisation and precariousness—where instrumentalism is actually a means to survive, while survival (and indeed success) might be seen as radical. From a more practical point of view, for communities experiencing cultural displacement due to the impacts of migration, craft and textile practices offer numerous possibilities— the ability to draw on existing cultural skills of making, for example, to generate income while preserving and passing on cultural knowledge. As Robertson and Vinebaum write, 'Textiles are passed down from one generation to another, connecting us to our families and communities, while the transmission of skills, such as weaving and dyeing, from parent to child also help to strengthen family bonds' (p. 3).

A growing number of social enterprises, therefore, are emerging globally that recognise these productive links between traditional skills and knowledge in textiles and craft (particularly evident in First Nations and migrant communities), with the manifest skills gaps in textile production in developed countries that have arisen as a result of significant shifts to offshore production. In the book *Sustainability and the Social Fabric: Europe's New Textile Industries* (2017), Paul Whittaker writes: 'An increasing number of start-up and more established textiles and fashion companies are taking an interest in combining entrepreneurial activity with the added value of traditional skills held in resettled immigrant communities' (Padovani & Whittaker, p. 9). Whittaker examines a number of examples of fashion-based social enterprises that bring together training and skills development in textile production with settlement support for migrant workers, including the UK enterprises Fashion Enter (London), Designer-Manufacturer Innovation Support Center (London) and Who Made Your Pants (Southampton). Further examples offered by Whittaker include the Australian enterprises The Social Studio (Melbourne) (to be discussed further in Chapter 5) and its sister organisation The Social Outfit (Sydney). Whittaker's analysis thus points to the positive potential for social enterprise, particularly in providing training that addresses industry skills gaps and pathways to employment for people from migrant backgrounds (Padovani & Whittaker, 2017).

The complexity of bringing together the goals of a fashion business with broader social goals, however, is not well understood in social enterprise scholarship. Case studies tend to focus on business models and organisational structures, while the lived experience of running these complex organisations with competing goals—financial, creative and social—is underrepresented. In the context of migration and settlement for migrant communities, structural and organisational barriers to employment are complex (Baker et al., 2021) and have important impacts on the types of outcomes that can be achieved by fashion-based social enterprises.

There are a range of settlement issues for people from migrant and refugee backgrounds which have commonality across countries. For migrant communities broadly, these include language barriers, lack of local networks (and resultant 'social capital') and cultural bias/racism which have particularly serious impacts on employment prospects (Baker et al., 2021). Language barriers also impact on educational attainment and outcomes. The lack of an extended network of family and friends has implications for social inclusion, wellbeing and practical issues like affordable childcare and access to temporary housing. For people from refugee backgrounds specifically, these issues are compounded with the devastating impacts of trauma (Kaplan, 2018). Trauma stems from a range of things: displacement, fear of safety, witnessing violence, medical issues, loss of loved ones, forced separation from family and friends, and negative experiences with authorities including police, military and government officials. These various traumas have long-term and long-ranging impacts on day-to-day life, including mental health and wellbeing, physical health, trust in relationships with peers, teachers and colleagues, and ability to concentrate and remember details. Flow-on effects in terms of education and work can include the need for greater flexibility in work hours or attendance, understanding of work absences to deal with health and family issues, the need for greater learning supports, building relationships and trust, and the creation of a safe and welcoming learning/working environment (Smith et al., 2020). Yet people from both migrant and refugee backgrounds depend on paid work—without social capital, financial means become even more important to securing livelihoods and futures. While some schools (admittedly not the majority) are able to address these needs, many, post-education workplaces are not equipped or structurally prepared to make these kinds of accommodations.

As a result, there are high levels of high school dropout for young people from migrant and refugee backgrounds, and even higher levels of unemployment (Thomas, 2016). While service providers often encourage refugee communities to find work in accessible industries, these can be poorly paid and often don't reflect long-term career aspirations (Oppedal et al., 2017). How then can young people from migrant and refugee backgrounds balance the pragmatic need to work and study with their rights to aspire to meaningful careers. And what are the opportunities for creative careers for those experiencing the forces of marginalisation—a central question addressed in this book? Angela McRobbie (2016) speaks to this idea of meaningful work when she discusses the motivations of small-scale fashion designers in Berlin:

> The [...] points to emphasize here include the reality of modest incomes on the part of the social entrepreneurs, the designers themselves and the fashion makers and crafters, indeed almost everyone across the fashion sector in the city. As Esther Perbandt said, "No one is making money." This in turn raises the question of what makes for a rewarding working life without the prospect of a large salary but with other compensatory rewards, such as a neighbourhood community that provides enjoyment and the pleasures of active citizenship and some sense of decision-making capacity and self-directed work. (p. 144)

Just as with other communities impacted by forces of marginalisation, creativity is a highly effective means to engage young people from refugee backgrounds, particularly those with low confidence in the traditional educational pillars of literacy and numeracy. Creative practices, craft and textile practices especially, are often accessible without prior knowledge—they thus provide a starting point of manual and creative skills and don't rely on high-level language skills. It is well recognised that material and aesthetic practices can generate alternative, richer forms of communication and expression beyond the verbal and can support the development of visual literacy and skills (de Leeuw & Rydin, 2007; Frimberger, 2016; Holzwarth & Maurer, 2001). Collaborative making practices also allow people to showcase and take pride in their creative skills, talents, prior knowledge and cultural backgrounds. This is particularly the case for people of migrant and refugee backgrounds because creative production attends to existing strengths and capacities, and has the potential to take the emphasis off language barriers and migratory experiences as deficits (Frimberger, 2016). Creative practices can also provide a means to reflect on social issues and offer cultural critique, and to transform subjectivities, for example from the migrant 'other' to a contemporary trend-setter, or from a deficit construction of identity towards a more empowered one.

Through the process of making in a textiles context, and building on already culturally embedded creative practices, training programs can develop a range of skills—from geometry and mathematics in the process of pattern-cutting to communication and expression through the translation of ideas into material form. Textile and craft forms tend towards collaboration or working in group settings—and can therefore enable the informal development of language skills through conversation, learning from peers and teachers, as well as the important twenty-first-century skill of *learning to learn*, as we discussed briefly in Chapters 2 and 3. As educational theorists Deakin et al. (2014) argue:

> More than ever before, the development of learning to learn is seen as crucial for success in the complex, unpredictable, and data-drenched world we share. Learning to learn is both a process and an outcome of formal education, together with other trans-disciplinary and lifewide competences. It goes deep into pedagogy and practice and is influenced

by culture and context. As an outcome, it is a competence we aspire to measure and celebrate. (p. 1)

Gaining confidence in a learning environment can encourage students/participants to explore other kinds of study—formal and informal. In the case of fashion-based social enterprises, skills also have direct relevance for industry—developing skills in sewing, garment construction, pattern making and so on can be applied in mainstream manufacturing settings.

It is perhaps this mix of vocational and creative skills that is of particular interest and value to young people from migrant and refugee backgrounds, who often face greater financial pressures and aspirations to work—both personally and from family (Oppedal et al., 2017). In a study of Arabic-speaking young creatives in Western Sydney, for example, Morgan and Idriss (2012) found that while many young people aspired to more ambitious or 'fashionable' creative paths, the majority curbed that ambition with pragmatic needs to find stable work. Likewise, in their study of refugee youth, Oppedal, Guribye and Kroger found a strong tendency to seek job security over personal aspiration. They write, 'In effect, most of them chose "safe" vocational paths toward earning a living rather than complex roads that led to the realization of their own long-term aspirations' (2017, p. 157). Of course, this has the danger of continuing the relegation of young creatives experiencing the impacts of marginalisation to 'production' rather than 'design' pathways—an issue that social enterprises face as well.

Given this emphasis on vocational paths, social enterprise as a model that prioritises job creation and economic return has proven successful in engaging migrant communities in creative work and careers (Kong, 2011). Moreover, as will be seen in the following chapter, some social enterprises can focus also on the development of design skills, alongside important and valuable craft skills. This balance, however, is not an easy one. Operating a social enterprise that has a social mission to support migrant and refugee communities requires, as discussed above, the provision of significant additional 'wrap-around' supports—from specialised training to social welfare support. For those working specifically with refugee communities, this also means the ability to provide flexibility and to adapt to a workforce with complex needs—all factors that impact on measures of business 'efficiency' and 'productivity' and on measures of training and employment transition outcomes.

Moreover, the fashion industry is a challenging setting for the operation of social enterprises—particularly those that need to implement a range of supports for their workers, or indeed are providing additional vocational training as part of their social mission. The rise of fast fashion and 'mega-brands', as discussed earlier in the chapter, has come at the expense of smaller brands and independent designers (McRobbie, 2016). In addition to the social impacts of this cannibalisation of market diversity, the increasing scale of these brands has brought ever more concerning environmental impacts and exacerbated the exploitation of labour—both through the use of low-paid workers in developing economies and the unethical use of migrant labour in economically developed nations (Gardetti & Torres, 2013; Payne, 2021). It is for this reason that it is important to consider the ways in which people from migrant and refugee communities in Western economies are active not only as producers of Western fashion, but are increasingly searching out opportunities to contribute at the level of design and entrepreneurial leadership. This tends to be more evident in grass-roots enterprises and through small business models led by creatives from migrant backgrounds—and less evident in the larger social enterprises and labels that attract public attention.

The flipside of this growth of big fashion, then, is the counterweight of growing interest in ethical, sustainable and community-oriented fashion labels that attempt to redress the sum of the global impacts of 'fast fashion'. This, in turn, provides opportunities for fashion-based social enterprises to potentially flourish. Such fashion-based social enterprises tend to be small scale, focused on providing ethical employment and often (but not always) pursue forms of environmental sustainability (McRobbie, 2016). Competing with larger brands, however, means developing products that either have much lower profit margins, or operate at the 'high end' of the market. Both approaches have inherent risk and face operational challenges to achieve financial sustainability. In her study of Berlin-based social enterprises, McRobbie advocates for the important social contribution that these small-scale enterprises can make to the urban fabric, even though they may seem to struggle financially. As McRobbie argues:

> Either we see the tiny outfits comprising two or three designers as inevitably under strain, and destined not to survive, or we can make a strong case for fashion to play an active role in developing possibilities for local urban employment and for contributing to a conversation about meaningful work. (2016, p. 119)

Adding to these financial challenges are the complex interactions of social and creative goals that drive many fashion-based SEs. Supporting the creative expression and development of emerging designers on the one hand and providing supportive training and work pathways on the other make for a challenging business model. So, how ambitious can fashion-based social enterprises be in expanding and developing their business operations while balancing these various goals? And likewise, what are the career prospects for young people from migrant and refugee backgrounds interested in fashion and design pathways? Current research on these questions is sparse, in both Australian and international contexts. Indeed, there is very little literature that addresses the lived experience of both the managers of fashion-based social enterprise and the communities of creatives for whom they are designed to support.

The next chapter will thus explore in greater depth the 'pragmatic ambitions' of fashion-based social enterprises, and the experiences and aspirations of young creatives working with them, through a detailed examination of our next case study organisation—The Social Studio: a fashion-based social enterprise based in Melbourne, Australia, that works with young people from migrant and refugee backgrounds through a fashion school, design label and manufacturing business.

References

Baker, S., Due, C., & Rose, M. (2021). Transitions from education to employment for culturally and linguistically diverse migrants and refugees in settlement contexts: What do we know? *Studies in Continuing Education, 43*(1), 1–15.

Bhachu, P. (2021). *Movers and makers: Uncertainty, resilience and migrant creativity in worlds of flux.* Taylor & Francis Group.

Deakin, C. R., Stringher, C., & Ren, K. (Eds.). (2014). *Learning to learn: International perspectives from theory and practice.* Taylor & Francis Group.

Dickens, L., & Lonie, D. (2013). Rap, rhythm and recognition: Lyrical practices and the politics of voice on a community music project for young people experiencing challenging circumstances. *Emotion, Space and Society, 9*, 59–71.

Frimberger, K. (2016). Towards a well-being focussed language pedagogy: Enabling arts-based, multilingual learning spaces for young people with refugee backgrounds. *Pedagogy, Culture & Society, 24*(2), 285–299.

Gardetti, M. A., & Torres, A. L. (2013). *Sustainability in fashion and textiles: Values, design, production and consumption.* Routledge.

Gibson, M. (2016). Weaving community together. In S. Butterwick & C. Roy (Eds.), *Working the margins of community-based adult learning: The power of arts-making in finding voice and creating conditions for seeing/listening* (pp. 27–38). SensePublishers.

Greer. (2014). *Craftivism: The art of craft and activism.* Arsenal Pulp Press.

Haraway. (2016). *Staying with the trouble: Making kin in the Chthulucene.* Duke University Press.

Holzwarth, P., & Maurer, B. (2001). Aesthetic creativity, reflexivity and the play with meaning: A video culture case study. *Journal of Educational Media, 26*(3), 185–202.

Hughes, C. (2012). Gender, craft labour and the creative sector. *International Journal of Cultural Policy, 18*(4), 439–454.

Kaplan, I. (2018). *Experiences of torture and trauma: Psychological and physical effects, management and psychological approaches.* The Australian Refugee Health Practice Guide. Accessed 15 December 2020, http://refugeehealthguide.org.au/wp-content/uploads/FINAL_BOOK_1_TORTURE_A4_web_FA.pdf

KNAG. (2021). *History*. Knitting Nanas Against Gas. Accessed 3 January 2021, https://knitting-nannas.com/about-us/history/

Kocher, A., & Stuesse, A. (2021). Undocumented activism and minor politics: Inside the cramped political spaces of deportation defense campaigns. *Antipode, 53*(2), 331–354.

Kong, E. (2011). Building social and community cohesion: The role of social enterprises in facilitating settlement experiences for immigrants from non-English speaking backgrounds. *The International Journal of Interdisciplinary Social Sciences, 6*(3), 115–128.

Leeuw, S. D., & Rydin, I. (2007). Migrant children's digital stories: Identity formation and self-representation through media production. *European Journal of Cultural Studies, 10*(4), 447–464.

McQuilten, G. (2017). The political possibilities of art and fashion based social enterprise. *Continuum, 31*(1), 69–83.

McQuilten, G. (2019). Who is afraid of public space? Public art in a contested, secured and surveilled city. *Art & the Public Sphere, 8*(2), 235–254.

McQuilten, G., & White, A. (2016). *Art as enterprise: Social and economic engagement in contemporary art*. I.B. Tauris.

McRobbie, A. (2016). *Be creative: Making a living in the new culture industries*. Polity Press.

Morgan, G., & Idriss, S. (2012). "Corsages on their parents' jackets": Employment and aspiration among Arabic-speaking youth in Western Sydney. *Journal of Youth Studies, 15*(7), 929–943.

Oppedal, B., Guribye, E., & Kroger, J. (2017). Vocational identity development among unaccompanied refugee minors. *International Journal of Intercultural Relations, 60*, 145–159.

Padovani, C., & Whittaker, P. (2017). *Sustainability and the social fabric: Europe's new textile industries*. Bloomsbury Publishing.

Payne, A. (2021). *Designing fashion's future: Present practice and tactics for sustainable change*. Bloomsbury Publishing.

Robertson, K., & Vinebaum, L. (2016). Crafting community. *TEXTILE, 14*(1), 2–13.

Shercliff, E. (2015). Joining in and dropping out: Hand-stitching in spaces of social interaction. *Craft Research, 6*(2), 187–207.

Shercliff, E., & Twigger Holroyd, A. (2016). Making with others: Working with textile craft groups as a means of research. *Studies in Material Thinking, 14*(paper 07), 1–17.

Smith, L., Hoang, H., Reynish, T., McLeod, K., et al. (2020). Factors shaping the lived experience of resettlement for former refugees in regional Australia.

International Journal of Environmental Research and Public Health, 17(501), 1–18.

Thomas, R. (2016). The right to quality education for refugee children through social inclusion. *Journal of Human Rights and Social Work, 1*(4), 193–201.

UNESCO. (2013). *Creative economy report*. United Nations Educational, Scientific and Cultural Organization. Accessed 15 August 2021, http://www.unesco.org/culture/pdf/creative-economy-report-2013.pdf

UNESCO. (2021). *Roadmap: International Year of creative economy for sustainable development*. United Nations Educational, Scientific and Cultural Organization. Accessed 3 January 2022, https://en.unesco.org/sites/default/files/creative_economy2021-unesco-roadmapen-ok2.pdf

5

The Social Studio: Hope and Pragmatic Ambition

Abstract For fashion-focused art-based social enterprises (ASEs), the notion of 'pragmatic ambitions' encapsulates their attempts to navigate the complexity of the global fashion market while prioritising social and ethical goals. This necessary pragmatism is explored in this chapter through the lens of our case study, The Social Studio (TSS): a social enterprise based in Australia that uses the vehicle of fashion to support educational and employment pathways for young creatives who have experienced migration and displacement. This chapter considers the tensions between commercial aspirations, as embedded in much ASE logic, and the realities of operating in ways that are counter to dominant business and cultural norms. Taking a deeper dive into the lived experience of students and staff at TSS, this chapter explores the ambivalent combination of ambition, hope and adaptability that characterises both the day-to-day running of the enterprise and the way that students engage with it in order to envisage their future. For the staff and emerging creatives involved at TSS, there are a number of recurring questions. For management, how does such an organisation constantly forge an enterprise that privileges social impact above all; how is success to be measured against conventional commercial and training benchmarks?

© The Author(s), under exclusive license to Springer Nature Switzerland AG 2022
G. McQuilten et al., *Art–Based Social Enterprise, Young Creatives and the Forces of Marginalisation*, https://doi.org/10.1007/978-3-031-10925-6_5

For students—who have variously experienced significant trauma, institutional barriers, language barriers and financial stress—what is a realistic hope for a future career in textile design and manufacture; is it the dream of opening a fashion label, or the more realistic step of finding some level of paid work in an aligned industry?

Keywords The social studio · Fashion · Art · Social enterprise · Craft · Textiles · Material practice · Employment · Education and training · Migration · Refugee experience

Introduction

It is a cool but sunny afternoon in the inner city of Melbourne, springtime. A small crowd has gathered in and around a laneway, which has become a makeshift fashion runway. There is a buzz in the air as designers gather with their friends and family, mixing with a diverse crowd of both dedicated fashionistas and curious onlookers, waiting for the show to begin. The parade features a mix of culturally diverse emerging designers, including The Social Studio (TSS) fashion label alongside one of TSS's successful graduates, Asia Hassan, who is presenting a capsule collection for her modest-wear label Asiyam. The event is simultaneously groundbreaking, yet somewhat low key, as models walk casually and quickly down the runway, and each of the labels represented is shown in fast succession. This is a key moment for Melbourne Fashion Week (MFW) in 2018. They are profiling culturally diverse and emerging designers as part of their main program—not as a side event. The event finishes with loud applause: but one designer is not happy. Asia had given express instructions that models were to be dressed with headscarves to recognise the label's objective to offer fashion-forward options for women who dress modestly—due to faith, religion or personal preference—but these directives were overlooked by the show's stylists. In an interview with Ruby Staley in *Fashion Journal* (2019), Asia reflected:

> On the day of the show, the models walked down the runway and I realised not a single one was wearing a headscarf. I was so heartbroken.

Everyone was congratulating me, but I was dying inside because I had lost all control.

Asia's experience speaks to the complexities of championing fashion informed by values of community and diversity in the context of an industry notorious for unscrupulous tactics, profiteering and homogeneity (Payne, 2021) (Fig. 5.1).

Fig. 5.1 Asia Hassan, *Take It Off!, 2019*. Asiyam Label (Image courtesy of Asiyam)

For fashion-focused art-based social enterprises, the notion of 'pragmatic ambitions' encapsulates their attempts to navigate the industry tactics, evident in Asia's example above and the complexity of the global fashion market while prioritising social and ethical goals. This necessary pragmatism is mirrored also in the lived experience of students engaged with our case study organisation: The Social Studio. This chapter considers the tensions between commercial aspirations, as embedded in much ASE logic, and the realities of operating in ways that are counter to dominant business and cultural norms. Taking a deeper dive into the lived experience of students and staff at TSS, this chapter explores the ambivalent combination of ambition, hope and adaptability that characterises both the day-to-day running of the enterprise and the way that students impacted by the effects of migration and displacement engage with it in order to envisage their future. For the staff and emerging creatives involved at TSS, there are a number of recurring questions. For management, how does such an organisation constantly forge an enterprise that privileges social impact above all; how is success to be measured against conventional commercial and training benchmarks? For students—who have variously experienced significant trauma, institutional barriers, language barriers and financial stress—what is a realistic hope for a future career in textile design and manufacture; is it the dream of opening a fashion label, or the more realistic step of finding some level of paid work in an aligned industry?

TSS is an ethical and sustainable fashion and design-based social enterprise that provides training and employment opportunities to people from migrant and refugee backgrounds through the vehicle of a vertical fashion business. It includes a manufacturing business, a retail shop, a clothing label and a fashion school where students learn sewing and design skills. One of the keys to the success of the TSS model is its combination of informal and formal learning processes, including both accredited Vocational Training (in the form of a Certificate III in Clothing Production) and non-accredited learning (social sewing, workshops, work experience programs, internships and pathway programs). This fosters an environment of co-making and co-producing through textiles as the foundation of TSS's work.

One of the first and most apparent aspects of the creative fashion-based learning model at TSS is its ability to engage and motivate students, including those who have had negative prior experiences of education and have been disengaged, or lack prior consistent schooling due to the dislocating effects of the migration experience. This reflects existing research observing the ways in which students from refugee backgrounds are engaged by creative learning activities that also foster positive social/community connections (Miralles-Lombardo et al., 2008; Thomas, 2016). As a result, the management and teaching staff at TSS report very high (over 90%) retention and completion rates. To put this into context, while there is limited research on educational retention rates for students from refugee backgrounds in Australia, the available literature (which reflects similar international data reported by the OECD) indicates a secondary school dropout rate of around 25% for these students, compared to 10% for Australian-born students (CMY, 2017; Gifford et al., 2009).

Coupled with the creativity involved in learning fashion-related skills, TSS offers a very flexible learning environment that is not overly strict about individual attendance, class times or group class work. This more accommodating approach suits students with different skill levels and external life pressures. As such, TSS's creative learning environment addresses less tangible issues such as confidence, social agency and community connection. Another key aspect of learning through sewing and 'making together' is the ability for students to teach each other, rather than relying on a more traditional or hierarchical teacher-student relationship. Indeed, a range of research notes that co-learning, skill sharing and mutual support is often an outcome of making textiles together (Gibson, 2016; Robertson & Vinebaum, 2016). The TSS model also reflects literature that indicates social enterprises can play a significant role in social cohesion through providing networked ecologies for, and with, new migrants to assist successful integration into the labour market. In this sense, social enterprises like TSS become, as Whittaker notes, 'the prime movers for achieving three key attributes for marginal groups: confidence, self-esteem, and emotional stability' (Padovani & Whittaker, 2017, p. 116). Furthermore, through integration into the world of work, Whittaker observes, 'employees who are otherwise marginalised can gain confidence and self-esteem that can transfer to their families and the extended community' (Padovani & Whittaker, 2017, p. 119).

Focusing, in particular, on this dynamic of networked ecologies, this chapter will look in greater detail at the lived experiences of both staff and students at TSS in order to understand the mechanics of using a creative learning environment to engage students who have experienced the impacts of migration and displacement. It will consider the kinds of unconventional pathways that this learning environment has provided, often into realms beyond the fashion industries, including examples of students starting up their own community enterprises. Finally, we will consider the ways in which students view their futures—as a way to unpack the complexity of pathways, transitions and ambitions for individuals (and their communities) experiencing the challenges of resettlement. These student perspectives shed light, in turn, on the pragmatic—and indeed, at times ambivalent—relationship that TSS has towards market forces more broadly—reflective of the complex conditions of ASEs operating with social goals in commercial markets.

The Learning Model at TSS

The make-up of students at TSS includes diverse ages, cultures, languages and genders. While fashion making and textile -making have been noted as being a largely female-led practice and industry (McRobbie, 2016; Shercliff, 2015), TSS has a number of male students, which reflects that in non-Western cultures men still frequently have professional roles as tailors in their communities. This points to an interesting gap in the literature on participatory textile making, which has tended to overlook non-Western histories and practices of making, where gender dynamics can look quite different to the Western context (Pain & Mallett, 2014; UNESCO, 2014).

As indicated above, creative and embodied approaches inform the organisational logic and pedagogical framework of TSS, where making together is a model of learning that addresses English as a Second

Language (ESL) issues and systemic barriers to education.[1] Apart from these more instrumental and measurable outcomes of such a model, often the point of traction for policy-makers and funders, we emphasise in this section the ways in which TSS's creative learning environment addresses less tangible issues such as confidence, social agency and community connection. A sense of engagement and motivation was articulated by many of the students who were interviewed for this study. For example, student Lila insisted 'I love doing this stuff. When you love something, you like to do everything. You finish quickly and you do more'.

From 2009 to 2020, TSS operated out of a storefront on busy Smith Street in Collingwood—one of Melbourne's oldest—and historically working class—inner urban areas. More recently, the store and school have relocated nearby to Collingwood Yards, a vibrant, new centralised hub of Melbourne creatives supported by affordable rents. While Collingwood is a trendy, quickly gentrifying inner suburb of Melbourne with rising rents, it is also central and conveniently located to five housing estates that service large communities from new migrant and refugee backgrounds. The suburb is also a short tram ride or walk from the city's Central Business District and is therefore easier to access for highly motivated students living in outer suburbs. Coming to a busy central location, with a thriving creative community, also enhances a sense of social connection and public participation for students and staff involved in TSS activities. This sense of bridging communities (a theme we will return to in Chapter 7) reflects similar findings about the role of social enterprise in connecting otherwise segregated minority communities in Scotland (Emejulu & Bassel, 2015). Nevertheless, while the central location serves local communities, as well as students who are willing and able to travel to attend TSS activities, it is less able to service other large migrant communities who have settled in the outer

---

[1] The importance of material and embodied making in the organisational logic of TSS, particularly in relation to language and cultural barriers, led to the authors embracing other, non-linguistic research methods for this case study, including observation of creative events hosted by TSS including a fashion parade and exhibition, and three of the research team participating in a weaving workshop alongside eight students, learning new skills together, and in the process discussing and experiencing how learning and creativity occur in cross-cultural, multilingual contexts at TSS.

suburbs of Melbourne and are unable to traverse the spatial divide (State of Victoria, 2011).

The TSS store sells a mixture of emerging local designers alongside items bearing the TSS label. These are displayed on racks of colourful, contemporary fashion, while above the store the site of the school and much of the manufacturing is visible and active. This sense of action and movement, used by other such enterprises, is particularly notable at TSS. As Angela McRobbie has noted, the visibility of such activity communicates to the customer 'the narratives of production' (2016, p. 132). At TSS, the store and the school space thus actively convey the organisation's approach to generating visibility for their diverse community of talented makers. As the organisation's website states:

> Part educator, part retailer, part production house and all about people, our not-for-profit social enterprise uses fashion and creativity to create work and learning opportunities for Melbourne's refugee and new migrant communities. (The Social Studio, 2019)

In underscoring this intended atmosphere, TSS manager Jean noted, 'It's really dynamic here, particularly with the shop, and so people come here and they can feel like they're part of something that's really successful, that isn't a daggy, drop-in centre'. Alongside TSS students who have dropped out of school and are disconnected from education, other students have lacked the opportunity to study due to the dislocating effects of the migration experience—and, as a result, they can highly prize and even valorize education. Student Jamal, for example, explained, 'Life is short, when learning is gone you're living for nothing. When you're living, there must be learning'. The ability to connect with both kinds of students—those disengaged due to previous schooling experiences, and those who are motivated but have limited prior learning experiences—speaks to the ways in which making, creating and producing can motivate and give confidence in a diverse learning context (Frimberger, 2016). Indeed, students at TSS often voiced that they had long been waiting for the opportunity to develop their skills in fashion and/or express their creativity, but hadn't found the right forum until they arrived at the Studio. It was not uncommon for students to express a sense of following their 'dream' (and we comment on this further, below). The impact of this high motivation within the TSS learning model is evidenced by what we have already noted as extremely high retention and completion rates, which TSS teaching staff themselves recognise is not necessarily due to their extraordinary efforts. As teacher Amanda told us, 'I've never really had anyone who's not genuinely interested, which I guess is pretty rare'.

Coupled with the creativity of learning fashion-related skills, TSS offers, as we have also previously noted, a very flexible learning environment. While there are approximately ten students enrolled in each of the two Certificate III programs offered, classes vary (day-to-day) between a few students and full capacity, with former students returning to use the machines and students from other classes joining in. This approach accommodates various skill and motivation levels and allows students to meet family and community obligations. It does, however, require teaching staff to be responsive to fluctuating class numbers and abilities. Student Niah spoke to this flexibility:

> It's good. I used to do VCE [secondary school] and now I can actually take my time and we have a lot of time to learn what we need to learn. So, there's no excuse at the end to not know how to do anything because we're not pressured at all.

The benefit of this lack of pressure was echoed by teacher Felicity, who explained:

> Some people need extra time. [...] you don't get lost in the classroom and fall behind. [...]. When you're comfortable, I think – they want to work, they want to come here, they want to do things, they want to learn, they're eager to learn. A lot of people, this is the first time they've ever studied.

As also previously signalled, a further key aspect of learning through sewing and making together is the ability for students to educate and train each other, rather than relying on the conventional teacher-student relationship. This reflects Robertson and Vinebaum's observation that collective textile-making activities can foster mutual support, build community and break social and cultural forms of isolation (2016). A number of the students at TSS talked of their willingness to help each other. Khemera, for example, said 'I put myself in that situation, and if anybody needs help, I will help them. I help them'. Speaking of how graduates and former students would often come to TSS during class time and work on their own individual projects, teacher Amanda further observed that despite the logistical challenges of the workspace at full capacity, this was ultimately a positive thing: 'And people end up learning off one another too. There's more skill sharing that goes on. So that helps nurture relationships'.

In the context of a migrant learning setting, addressing and overcoming ESL is a crucial aspect of the creativity-led teaching approach. Student Yasaman spoke to the ways in which art-making transcends these barriers when she said 'Art is different. It's all about what you're making, you create something. [The language] is not much of an issue'. Nevertheless, TSS relies on volunteers to provide additional, one-on-one ESL tuition for students, as teaching staff can struggle to find time in class to support students individually with written work. What emerged across the interviews with students was their need for a supportive training environment specifically designed for people with varied levels of English, rather than a more mainstream or general creative/fashion-based training program. This reflects Loshini Naidoo's (2015) research on refugee educational outcomes, evidencing the need to create supportive environments, where teachers are aware of the learning differences of students from refugee backgrounds, in order to foster greater confidence in learning. In other words, creativity in and of itself isn't the answer to their educational barriers—but creativity, in conjunction with a supportive ESL learning environment, becomes a powerful combination. Yasaman described this effect:

> You know, I haven't had enough confidence to start because this is my third language and I couldn't talk well, but they didn't care. They didn't care where you are coming from, if you can talk English or not. They're really patient to try to understand what you are trying to say.

Indeed, at TSS, language and the materiality of textiles become a joint communicative medium. The ability for fashion in particular to cross cultural barriers was expressed by teacher Amanda when she explained:

> The students bring in textiles from their home country to make a garment out of. Because clothing is so universal, everyone has a story about clothing and about textiles – it really is very inclusive and every culture has something to offer.

This co-making—and highly material—environment that attends to cultural barriers was also observed by the authors of this book during a participatory yarn weaving workshop led by TSS alumni and Somalian weaver Muhubo Sulieman. As we, along with a group of TSS students, were shown customary Somali finger weaving techniques, talk naturally moved to the subject of yarning wool and another student showed us photos on her phone of the yaks that she used to herd in Tibet. Consequently, she started teaching us how to spin wool with our fingers the way she had been taught at home, and Muhubo was again a student, learning a new set of weaving techniques. Through this unexpected and generous sharing, we encountered the textile, embodied, material pedagogy that underpins the logic of TSS (McQuilten & Spiers, 2020) (Figs. 5.2 and 5.3).

This encapsulates a key aspect of the TSS environment. What emerged variously through our interviews with students at TSS—and that is specific to creative practice and the making of textiles—was a sense of increased confidence to try new things, which then flows on to interests in further study and careers. When we asked students about their pathways and futures, however, the focus was not necessarily on ambitious creative careers as fashion designers or artists—and it is to these futures that we now turn.

Fig. 5.2 Muhubo Sulieman leads a weaving workshop at The Social Studio in August 2019 (Photograph Teva Cosic)

Pragmatic Ambitions—Hope Meets Reality

When asked about their hopes and plans for the future, a number of students at TSS expressed a general positivity about the future, a desire to complete their Certificate III program, a strong sense of community and an interest in sharing their skills and helping people. Azadeh, for example, simply talked about their ability to make things, saying 'I'm excited for the future. I'm so excited to make new garments and different things'. Khemera, meanwhile, talked about using her skills to help others: 'I would like in my future if I could, I want to be a designer for a lot of people. I'd love to have a lot of people that if I could, using my opportunity and my experience'.

While the formal vocational training at TSS focuses on clothing production, this is not necessarily the full scope of creative training and learning that takes place. As staff member Pierre described, 'We show them there's more than just making clothes […] Between the show we're doing, you can be a stylist, you can be a machinist, you can be a textile

5 The Social Studio: Hope and Pragmatic Ambition

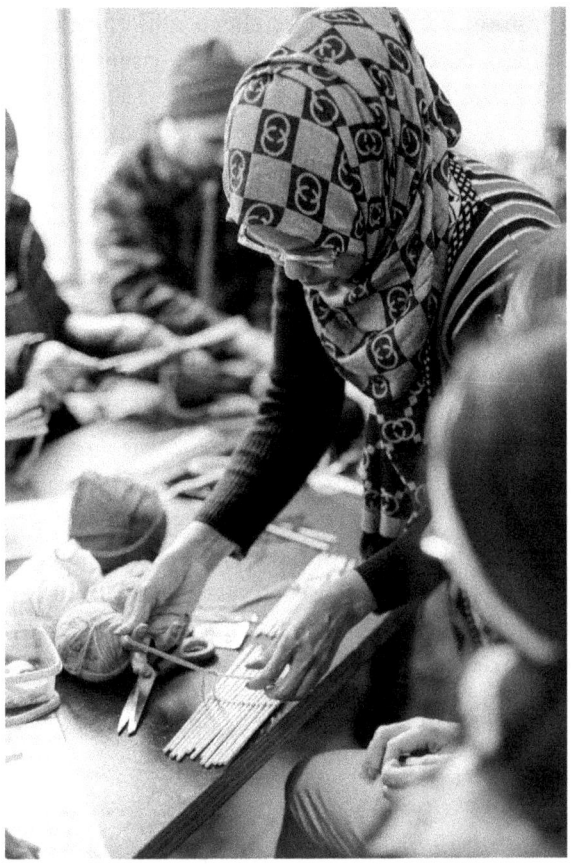

Fig. 5.3 Muhubo Sulieman instructs one of the researchers and a student of The Social Studio how to do finger weaving in August 2019 (Photograph Teva Cosic)

designer, you can be a photographer'. This challenges the focus of the vocational education system in Victoria, where VET training in clothing production (as opposed to a university degree in fashion and textiles) merely offers practical (and state funded) pathways into work in manufacturing. Lack of access to other kinds of study in fashion and textiles is thus a potential barrier for young people undertaking VET courses, making it difficult for them to transition into more diverse careers in the industry. As staff member India noted, 'If you want to go and do fashion at a fashion school, it's not cheap and there's no subsidies or anything'. Perhaps partly as a result of these issues in accessing higher education in fashion, both students and staff at TSS talked about a range of career pathways emerging out of their engagement with the Studio, from careers in fashion to starting up their own businesses, often beyond fashion and textiles. As Khemera explained:

> I wanted to be a big designer before, but you have to study many degrees, many levels. So my own shop – that's what I want [...] For now, whatever opportunity that I have, I will grab.

Despite these various positive aspirations for the future, it was notable across the interviews that students at TSS, compared to young people engaged with other case study ASEs, were more pragmatic in their thinking about the future. This isn't to suggest that they didn't have ambitions, or that they didn't see pathways in the creative industries. Rather, when students at TSS talked about 'next steps', they were noticeably practical steps, such as going from a Certificate III program to a Certificate IV or developing a business as additional income to a more stable job. Niah, for example, told us:

> Firstly, I just want to improve my skills with the resources I have, like at The Social Studio. And then after that buy a sewing machine, focus on that [...] And then maybe with that, I'll make garments rather than mending them [...] Start with my family at home. And then if that works out, other people of course will find out. And then maybe start my own business if it does work out from somewhere based in the community [...] I'll make some garments to be sold in little stores [...] If that works out then I'll also have my own shop where I only sell my own things, then I guess become a well known designer. But if all of that doesn't happen, just being here is also fine for me.

This reflects a broader research literature on the work futures of young people from migrant and refugee backgrounds, who tend to look towards 'realistic' or less precarious pathways into work. Even for those with greater opportunity to enter a professional career, this emphasis on the practical remained. This was partly due, in the case of young creatives

5 The Social Studio: Hope and Pragmatic Ambition

at TSS, to familial perceptions of the creative industries—with families encouraging careers in other industries like accounting, medicine and law—and partly due to the pressures on young people to earn and maintain income to support themselves and their (often extended) families. Student Azadeh, for example, commented that her Persian parents had hoped she would pursue a career in medicine, business, law or architecture, while Niah noted her parents wanted her to have a 'Plan B' to fashion, which had led her to study a bachelor degree in health science.

In a study of young creatives from Arabic-speaking backgrounds in Australia, George Morgan and Sheren Idriss described these same tensions between career desires and work realities. As they noted:

> What these case studies illustrate is the sense of turmoil confronting many emerging adults facing choices around work and education. While they formulate ambitions that are less conventional (than for example a manual trade or accountancy), most end up directing their careers in safe and conformist ways, often by abandoning the creative fulfilment they were initially seeking. (2012, p. 940)

Besides the exigencies of career choice, staff at TSS also identified significant barriers for students in transitioning to work and further study, including the ongoing impacts of language and literacy barriers, and the cost of further education. Staff member, India, expressed frustration at this dilemma:

> You want to be instilling in them, "you can do whatever you want and we're going to support you to do that", but at the end of the day, there are some big limitations to actually accessing that kind of education, even if it is based in creativity and skills that they actually already have. If they don't have the literacy skills, it's difficult.

Perhaps even more pressing was the sense of ambivalence, carried by a number of teaching staff, towards the global fashion industry itself. The industry logic of exploitation, hyperconsumption and waste raised concerns about what this meant for TSS graduates. Focusing on ethical and sustainable fashion helps address this dilemma, but also reduces the scale of work opportunities—as India explained:

> I think the fashion industry and the manufacturing industry in Australia is a tricky one. Especially the ethical fashion scene in Australia is very narrow and small. So they don't have a lot of space for movement. So [it's about] connecting in with that and making sure we're doing the best for our students.

Here manifests a key tension in the values of TSS between pragmatism—helping their communities to get jobs in the industry—and ambition—trying to transform the industry itself into a more socially just and sustainable one. Students reflect a similar tension in their goals to find practical work and practical pathways, which are set against their creative hopes and ambitions.

TSS students have also responded to these challenges by starting up their own enterprises, including a few that have replicated the model of TSS within their own communities. Abuk Bol, for example, a graduate and former manufacturing employee, went on to start the Twich Women's Sewing Collective in 2012—a community enterprise run entirely by women from the Twich language group of the South Sudanese community in Melbourne (McQuilten, 2017) (Fig. 5.4). Another, Francess Sesay, started up a similar community enterprise called Kontiki Fashions that works with migrant women in the Western suburbs of Melbourne (Capone, 2015). It's notable that both of these examples have stronger social and community goals than financial ones and like TSS, tend to resist or challenge aspects of mainstream fashion and enterprise by providing opportunities for workers who lack prior skills and experience, by promoting values of ethical labour and operating in ways that privilege collective value over individual gains.

In addition to those young creatives who, like Abuk and Francess, had a clear focus on practical work and study goals, other students at TSS were unsure entirely of what their work futures might hold. As teacher Amanda observed:

> Some people are very driven and they have a very good idea of what they want to get out of the course and what the next steps are, and other people have no idea and they're a bit fearful about the future.

5 The Social Studio: Hope and Pragmatic Ambition 97

Fig. 5.4 Twich Women's Sewing Collective founder Abuk Bol (far right) with co-founders (left to right) Nyachol John, Ayen Bol and Akech Majok (Image courtesy of Twich Women's Sewing Collective)

Amanda went on to explain that they try to gently support those more uncertain students to find their aspirations. At TSS, this individualised approach to pathways has meant that students have transitioned into a broad range of careers, both in and beyond the creative industries, including, for example, work in health, hospitality, legal professions, accounting and international development. In this way, the initial creative engagement of the programs at TSS supports students to 'learn to learn' (as was the case at Youthworx) and to build what might be considered 'soft skills' or twenty-first-century skills, while building networks, professional communities and confidence to consider further work and study options. As student Yasaman insisted: 'I'm planning to improve my English and start higher education […] I'm going to go for Certificate IV and get enough confidence to go for a Bachelor degree'.

There was also a generational aspect to the focus on pathways, with younger people focused on short-term work goals or unsure about work entirely, while older people had clearer long-term focus on finding meaningful work. As staff member Pierre observed:

> If you're talking about an older person, for them, it's more about getting work. But if we're talking about a young generation, it's more about the coming in [to experience TSS] because they don't really know what's out there. You don't know what you're going to do.

This idea of 'coming in' speaks to the simplicity of having a community to *make with* and to *be with*. A recurrent theme throughout the interviews was that of past students and graduates returning to TSS (which, as we noted earlier, also facilitated informal learning). As teacher Felicity noted, 'I haven't met anyone that's graduated and never came back. All the ones that I have met that graduated last time, I've seen them all again'—a comment that speaks of connection as much as learning. Indeed, TSS privileges the creation of a space of belonging and welcome, which creates a complex juggle to also support the practical requirements of running a business, such as productivity and efficiency. The value and importance of a space that is welcoming and supportive for young people from refugee backgrounds, however, can't be underestimated. As Pierre explained:

> The main outcome of coming to The Social Studio is you have a space where it's a safe house. [...] It's one of those places where when you come in, it's more than just coming into school. It's about coming to a place where let's do stuff from 11 o'clock to 4 o'clock, you won't have to think about how your situation is.

Fashioning Enterprise at TSS

The conundrum of transitioning TSS students into the fashion industry, marked by a deeply problematic record on a range of issues from social justice to ecological impacts, speaks to a central challenge for TSS itself, trying to operate a viable fashion enterprise in the context of an industry that thrives on the exploitation of labour and is extractive and wasteful of resources (Gardetti & Torres, 2013). Most of the teachers and retail/manufacturing staff at TSS, for example, have come directly from the fashion industry—which they view through a critical lens. As Pierre commented:

> I actually didn't want to work in the industry anymore [...] You know, you made this piece which is amazing. It was a success. You sold it. And because it's next season, you need to make more and more money, it's just 50,000 pieces of that unsold. Where are they going to go?

Similarly, staff member Neika, who had left the mainstream fashion industry, was excited about the opportunity to use her business skills in a social enterprise context 'that wasn't about making people rich, that had a greater purpose to it'.

Along with greater purpose, however, comes greater complexity. TSS has to produce products that can compete with the diversity and speed of mainstream fashion, at a price point that can cover ethical wages (in the case of TSS, accredited by Ethical Clothing Australia and audited by the Textile Union), and can finance the significant overheads of training and supporting staff from complex backgrounds. The TSS fashion label works with up-cycled fabrics from industry, which reduces both the types and quantities of fabrics available to produce products. Consumers expecting, for example, to order a size M in blue may simply not have those options when they shop at TSS. A further challenge is how to market TSS products in a way that appeals to a fashion-savvy audience, but explains the additional social and environmental value of the products (and explains also the higher price points). Pierre noted:

> You're designing but you're designing with a purpose. And there's "how do you market it and how do you sell it" but also explaining to people the social aspect of it rather than just saying, "Oh, this is a T-shirt." No, it's not just a T-shirt. This T-shirt feeds X in family. And the reason for paying X for this T-shirt is this, this, this, this. And I think that's what a lot of people forget about.

Telling these stories in the context of a retail pitch also requires nuance and critical reflection—it can be all too easy for 'storytelling' to stigmatise the very communities that TSS works with. Emejulu and Bassel

(2015) have noted, for example, that minority and migrant communities of colour—with their study dealing in particular with Muslim women—are frequently only seen and heard in the public sphere if they are constructed as vulnerable and passive victims in need of help or if they play the role of productive and deserving neoliberal citizens, or 'good migrants', who speak the language of hard work, entrepreneurship and innovation. While TSS is very aware of these issues, they are also aware of the power of storytelling to appeal to funders and industry partners and thus the need to present narratives of transformation, especially to funders, while not fetishising this aspect of people's lives in terms of deficit and impairment. This speaks to Elyse Gordon's (2013) analysis of the challenges of operating youth programs in a neoliberal context, where stories of individual transformation have become the essential fuel for philanthropy and donor support. As Gordon argues:

> Organizations rely on donors who are collectively informed by dominant poverty knowledge that, when paired with imaginaries about 'successful youth', promote practices that reify discourses of deservingness and teach individual skills that elide any attention to structural inequalities. (p. 114)

Shifting focus away from the individual story of transformation and towards systemic change is therefore a significant challenge for ASEs that rely on philanthropic funding to survive.

In addition to managing these tensions between business growth, funding and social mission, the day-to-day operations of TSS require great agility and a range of skills from staff. For example, a central requirement for engaging diverse students from migrant and refugee backgrounds at TSS is flexibility; we have already discussed the need for flexibility around attendance for students, and in addition, there are the challenges of welcoming a range of past and current students and staff simultaneously and adapting to the skills of students at different stages of a study program (e.g. one might be in their first semester and another in their last). Alongside these training issues, staff need to respond to day-to-day organisational needs—whether it be guiding a tour of students from a local high school or responding to a sudden large order that requires teaching staff to multitask in the often busy workspace available. TSS teacher Amanda gives a sense of how this day-to-day flexibility manifests in both challenges and opportunities:

> Because we have an open door policy too, we have graduates who are very much welcome to come back in and we also have people that are studying in other places who come in for assistance. So it might be one day where you've got literally 20 people or 15 people all working in a very, very cosy space and you just think oh my God [...] You're just kind of running around in a flap. But that's also really energising. [...] I've never really had many students complain about it being too busy because it just does bring a real nice buzz and energy and vibrancy. And people end up learning off one another too. There's more skill sharing that goes on. So that helps nurture relationships.

Offering holistic support and wrap-around services to students and staff who have been impacted by migration and displacement means that teachers can inadvertently find themselves in multiple roles as counsellors, advisors and career mentors. This has been addressed in recent times by TSS bringing in additional resources including, for example, a Youth Pathways Coordinator, and providing professional development for teaching staff in relation to the mental health needs of students from refugee backgrounds. What these additional supports indicate, however, is that ASEs cannot be compared to conventional businesses concerned predominantly with economic outputs. When trying to support the specific needs of diverse communities, TSS, like other ASEs, faces the need to divert considerable resources away from core business in terms of production and sales. For example, funding new positions such as that of the Youth Pathways Coordinator is unlikely to generate financial return to the organisation. In order to maintain this adaptability and focus on social mission, TSS, as with so many ASEs, draws income from diverse sources beyond trade including donations, sponsorship and philanthropy, in turn providing different kinds of non-economic value to the community. In doing so, ASEs often align with other forms of alternative and ethical enterprise to potentially offer powerful models of 'doing business' differently, especially in terms of rethinking what the generation of 'value' in a business might look like.

Conclusion

Making textiles together is understood widely to facilitate communication and exchange and foster social bonds (Gibson, 2016; Robertson & Vinebaum, 2016; Shercliff, 2015; Shercliff & Twigger Holroyd, 2016), and this was certainly evident at TSS. In the organisation's pedagogical method, its creative events and activities, and in its day-to-day operations, we witnessed the ways in which conversation, cooperation and mutuality were generated through co-making. It is also pertinent to reiterate that making together in this context did not privilege the verbal. Creative practice facilitated the 'being together' of an intercultural and diverse group of people, allowing the development of rapport, helping each other and creative expression without the need for strong skills in a single language.

Our findings therefore support existing literature that argues that creative methods enable people to communicate through non-verbal means, while co-making slows the pace of conversation and produces time to reflect before verbalising an opinion (Gauntlett, 2007; Shercliff & Twigger Holroyd, 2016). This is especially significant for young people, and people impacted by forces of migration and displacement, who might have different approaches to communication and reflection, or who grapple with language barriers. This does not mean communication is reduced. On the contrary, it is well evidenced that visual, material and aesthetic practices can generate alternative, richer forms of communication and expression (Holzwarth & Maurer, 2001; Leeuw & Rydin, 2007)—and this is certainly evident within TSS. Collaborative making practices also allow people from migrant and refugee backgrounds to showcase and take pride in their creative skills, and in their prior knowledge and cultural backgrounds without placing emphasis on the language barrier and migratory past experience as deficits (Frimberger, 2016; McQuilten & Spiers, 2020; McQuilten, 2017).

Herein lies a paradox at the heart of TSS, which speaks to tensions in ASEs more generally. By harnessing the power of creativity to generate practical outcomes (skills development and income generation) for young people who have experienced migration and displacement, TSS shows the potential of arts programs to generate social value. Yet ASEs

5 The Social Studio: Hope and Pragmatic Ambition

like TSS are measured against much more concrete measures of profit-generation and volumes of people transitioning into work and further study. This imperative to achieve growth in order to meet the expectations of the SE sector and present and future funders was evident, for example, when staff member Neika described the potential of TSS opening a new site for training in Heidelberg West, a Northern suburb of Melbourne with large populations of new migrants:

> We have access to a space in West Heidelberg that is peppercorn rent. It will allow us to have a satellite location [...] so we can actually open up a second school which is really great because we can expand that reach [...] The dream scenario would be the digital print [studio] would live there and we could either have the current course there or even revive the textile design course which'd be really, really great. So there's that group opportunity and expanding that kind of reach and impact is a really great thing for funding, because there's growth, which is what funders want to see.

While TSS certainly achieves results in the more quantifiable areas of employment and educational outcomes, particularly in terms of educational attainment, our research has observed that the more significant impacts can be seen in the improvements in wellbeing and social inclusion for those young creatives involved—which are, as we argue, the essential precursors to transitioning into further work and study.

In order to survive at this cross-section of social welfare and commercial enterprise, TSS has had to be pragmatic in its ambitions—both in its ambitions to compete (and potentially transform) the conditions of the fashion industry and in its ambitions to achieve scalable measures of social impact (e.g. high rates of employment outcomes for funders). Likewise, TSS students are naturally tempering their creative ambitions in carving out pathways that are achievable within the structural limitations of a society that struggles to recognise prior learning and work experience for newly arrived migrants and which imposes significant barriers (financial, racial/cultural and social) to accessing both mainstream education and work. Yet in the midst of these pragmatic challenges, creativity is alive and thriving, as described by TSS teacher India:

The exciting thing is [students] can see themselves creating this product and it's actually something that's useful and they've used creative and artistic skills to get to that point, as well. So it's that freedom of expression, as well, that's important.

By providing this platform for artistic expression, along with a space for material and embodied learning—and simply a place to 'come to'—TSS enacts a radical alternative to the numbers-driven, scale-focused and unsustainable tenets of the mainstream fashion industry. In doing so, it stands as a model for community enterprising that supports access to employment and education for communities impacted by the forces of migration and displacement.

References

Capone, A. (2015). Kontiki Cultural Women Empowerment group inspires migrant women in Melbourne's west. *Brimbank Leader Newspaper*, July 21. Accessed 15 September 2021, https://www.heraldsun.com.au/leader/news/kontiki-cultural-women-empowerment-group-inspires-migrant-women-in-melbournes-west/news-story/87d776a1262b1def921a9537855f68b8

CMY. (2017). *Settlement outcomes of young people from refugee and migrant backgrounds: A submission to the Federal Government's Inquiry into Settlement Outcomes—Australian Senate Inquiry Report*. Carlton: Centre for Multicultural Youth. Accessed 9 April 2020 and 22 January 2022, https://www.aph.gov.au/DocumentStore.ashx?id=4189091b-dac6-4895-8b75-ea9f92aecce1&subId=463724

Emejulu, A., & Bassel, L. (2015). Minority women, activism and austerity. *Race & Class, 57*(2), 86–95.

Frimberger, K. (2016). Towards a well-being focussed language pedagogy: Enabling arts-based, multilingual learning spaces for young people with refugee backgrounds. *Pedagogy, Culture & Society, 24*(2), 285–299.

Gardetti, M. A., & Torres, A. L. (2013). *Sustainability in fashion and textiles: Values, design, production and consumption*. Routledge.

Gauntlett, D. (2007). *Creative explorations: New approaches to identities and audiences*. Routledge.

Gibson, M. (2016). Weaving community together. In S. Butterwick & C. Roy (Eds.), *Working the margins of community-based adult learning: The power of arts-making in finding voice and creating conditions for seeing/listening* (pp. 27–38). Sense Publishers.

Gifford, S., Correa-Velez, I., & Sampson, R. (2009). *Good starts for recently arrived youth with refugee backgrounds: Promoting wellbeing in the first three years of settlement in Melbourne, Australia*. La Trobe Refugee Research Centre.

Gordon, E. (2013). Under-served and un-deserving: Youth empowerment programs, poverty discourses and subject formation. *Geoforum, 50*, 107–116.

Holzwarth, P., & Maurer, B. (2001). Aesthetic creativity, reflexivity and the play with meaning: A video culture case study. *Journal of Educational Media, 26*(3), 185–202.

Leeuw, S. D., & Rydin, I. (2007). Migrant children's digital stories: Identity formation and self-representation through media production. *European Journal of Cultural Studies, 10*(4), 447–464.

McQuilten, G. (2017). The political possibilities of art and fashion based social enterprise. *Continuum, 31*(1), 69–83.

McQuilten, G., & Spiers, A. (2020). 'Art is different': Material practice, learning and co-making at the social studio. *Journal of Arts & Communities, 10*(1/2), 19–33.

McRobbie, A. (2016). *Be creative: Making a living in the new culture industries*. Polity Press.

Miralles-Lombardo, B., Miralles, J., & Golding, B. (2008). *Creating learning spaces for refugees: The role of multicultural organisations in Australia*. NCVER.

Morgan, G., & Idriss, S. (2012). "Corsages on their parents' jackets": Employment and aspiration among Arabic-speaking youth in Western Sydney. *Journal of Youth Studies, 15*(7), 929–943.

Naidoo, L. (2015). Educating refugee-background students in Australian schools and universities. *Intercultural Education, 26*(3), 210–217.

Padovani, C., & Whittaker, P. (2017). *Sustainability and the social fabric: Europe's new textile industries*. Bloomsbury Publishing.

Pain, A., & Mallett, R. (2014, July). *Gender, youth and urban labour market participation: Evidence from the tailoring sector in Kabul, Afghanistan* (SLRC Working Paper 18). Secure Livelihoods Research Consortium, pp. i–30.

Payne, A. (2021). *Designing fashion's future: Present practice and tactics for sustainable change*. Bloomsbury Publishing USA.

Robertson, K., & Vinebaum, L. (2016). Crafting community. *TEXTILE, 14*(1), 2–13.

Shercliff, E. (2015). Joining in and dropping out: Hand-stitching in spaces of social interaction. *Craft Research, 6*(2), 187–207.

Shercliff, E., & Twigger Holroyd, A. (2016). Making with others: Working with textile craft groups as a means of research. *Studies in Material Thinking, 14*(Paper 07), 1–17.

The Social Studio. (2019). *The social studio website: About us.* Accessed 14 October 2021, https://www.thesocialstudio.org/about-us/

Staley, R. (2019, November). Asia Hassan on what diversity really means to Australian fashion. *Fashion Journal.* Accessed 4 January 2022, https://fashionjournal.com.au/fashion/muslim-designer-asia-hassan-writing-rules-fashion/

State of Victoria. (2011). *Refugee status report: A report on how refugee children and young people in Victoria are faring.* Department of Education and Early Childhood Development, Victorian Government. Accessed 9 April 2020, https://www.education.vic.gov.au/about/research/Pages/reportdatarefugee.aspx

Thomas, R. (2016). The right to quality education for refugee children through social inclusion. *Journal of Human Rights and Social Work, 1*(4), 193–201.

UNESCO. (2014). *Gender equality, heritage and creativity.* United Nations Educational, Scientific and Cultural Organization. Accessed 9 April 2021, http://www.unesco.org/new/en/culture/gender-and-culture/gender-equality-and-culture/the-report/

6

Creative Practice, Cultural Citizenship and the Urban Fringe

Abstract This chapter considers the ways in which local, situated experience, along with class background and socio-economic status, influences the aspirations, values and career motivations of young people involved in art-based social enterprises. In recognising the socio-spatial changes brought about by gentrification and suburbanisation, including the displacement of communities to the urban fringe, a number of art-based social enterprises (ASEs) internationally attempt to address locational disadvantage through engaging young people living in the urban fringe in various forms of creative practice. One notable emphasis has been on performance, dance and music projects—thus leveraging the greater engagement of young people with these contemporary art forms. Indeed, the performing arts provide a ready platform for individual storytelling, cultural expression and opportunities for income generation that can be attractive to young people impacted by forces of marginalisation. While such ASE interventions are often constructive and purposeful, they can also be couched in terms of a transformational narrative where an individual who has experienced socio-economic hardship overcomes personal circumstances and barriers to achieve normative goals of creative success or, at least, recognition. The key question explored in this chapter is whether such a narrative—and the ASE activity that fosters it—might also tend to mask the very structural inequities, displacements and marginalities that characterise life on the urban fringe.

Keywords Urban fringe · Gentrification · Spatial disadvantage · Performing arts · Art · Social enterprise · Young creatives · Employment · Storytelling · Transformation

Introduction

This chapter considers the ways in which local, situated experience, along with class background and socio-economic status, influences the aspirations, values and career motivations of young people involved in ASEs. There is a long recognised relationship between the gentrification of inner urban areas and the subsequent displacement of established communities—often ones experiencing forms of social and economic marginalisation—to the urban fringe (Eckardt, 2021). Tracking alongside this displacement has been the increasing spatialisation of disadvantage, as suburbanisation takes increasing hold in large cities across the globe (such that a postcode, for example, increasingly becomes a predictor of health and wellbeing outcomes). What is perhaps less well recognised is that artistic practice has been implicated in this urban change, especially through creatives and creative industries moving into inner city areas, thereby stimulating cultural and economic activity, and attracting business development (Tunalı, 2021).

In recognising this socio-spatial change, a number of ASEs internationally attempt to address this locational disadvantage—and the inner urban conglomeration of creative production—through engaging young people living in the urban fringe in various forms of creative practice. One notable emphasis has been on performance, dance and music projects—thus leveraging the greater engagement of young people with these contemporary art forms. Indeed, the performing arts provide a ready platform for individual storytelling, cultural expression and opportunities for income generation that can be attractive to young people impacted by forces of marginalisation. While such ASE interventions are often constructive and purposeful, they can also be couched in terms of a transformational narrative where an individual who has experienced socio-economic hardship overcomes personal circumstances and barriers to achieve normative goals of creative success or, at least, recognition. The key question explored in this chapter is whether such a narrative—and the ASE activity that fosters it—might also tend to mask the very structural inequities, displacements and marginalities that characterise life on the urban fringe.

There is a considerable body of literature on the historic connections between artists and gentrification in American and European cities, particularly emerging out of the counter-cultural movements of the 1970s, where artists moved into poorer inner urban neighbourhoods and established hubs of artistic practice that combined aesthetic and social justice interests (Lindner & Sandoval, 2021). More recently, urban developments, picking up on this historical phenomenon, now routinely seek to include cultural precincts in urban design as a means to foster the economic improvement of urban areas through cultural activity that attracts audiences and customers and strengthens real estate markets. Intentionally or not, this often contributes to a displacement of lower socio-economic community groups, forced to leave for outer suburbs due to rising rents and class displacement. This marginalisation and dispersal of 'traditional' inner urban communities are deeply connected, within many Australian cities (as elsewhere) to both ethnicity and race. In *Art & gentrification in the changing neoliberal landscape* (2021), Tijen Tunali discusses these relations between artist practices, urban development and the displacement of (lower socio-economic) residents due to gentrification:

> Residents who live in the areas for urban redevelopment are forced to relocate due to rising rental prices, high costs of nearby facilities and an overall sense of being unwelcome. Class privileges are central to this spatial restructuring; thus, gentrification can be recognized as the intensification of class and ethnic divides through the movement of capital. (p. 6)

Nevertheless, the relationship between artists and these forces of gentrification and displacement are nuanced: artists are often displaced themselves by the eventual forces of gentrification and rising rents, while artists also have the potential to organise politically and resist some of these forces in partnership with impacted community groups (Rich, 2019).

Andrew Harris (2012) describes this tension in relation to histories of gentrification in the UK, with a specific focus on the deindustrialised and subsequently gentrified neighbourhood of Hoxton in London in the 1990s. While acknowledging that artists have been complicit in forces of gentrification that have erased social histories of class and ethnicity, Harris argues that there is also a role for artists in highlighting and potentially resisting these very forces of gentrification. Giving examples of recent artists who have collaborated with communities impacted by urban change such as Melanie Manchot and Laura Oldfield Ford, Harris writes:

> Artistic interventions such as these offer an important and neglected resource for complicating, disrupting and re-visioning understandings of urban change (see also Pinder 2008). It is through these more critical cultural reframings of social and political urban relations, especially in the context of periods of economic downturn, that potential new waves of gentrification in cities such as London can begin to be refigured and resisted. (2012, p. 14)

Importantly for this chapter, Harris is particularly drawn to artistic practices that engage with specific histories of places impacted by urban development.

In much urban sociological scholarship, an understanding of the specific socio-economic transformations of particular geographic places is crucial to understanding the broader impacts of urban development in terms of social change, particularly in relation to rapid growth in urban populations and the resulting phenomenon of 'city sprawl'. As we have begun to discuss above, the rapid economic development and spatial expansion of cities in the twenty-first century has shifted patterns of economic and social advantage, in particular resulting in growing urban 'fringe' areas with lower-income communities that experience various forms of economic and social disadvantage. As Martin and Goodman (2016) explain:

> As the cities have continued to expand outwards, a significant issue of housing affordability has pushed low-income families to the urban fringe. There is growing concern that the physical distance from central cities is creating new forms of exclusion and disadvantage. (p. 236)

As a result, Martin and Goodman argue for a more spatial understanding of disadvantage and for concomitant shifts in social work policy and practice that can attend to the particular needs of communities displaced to the urban fringe and that take into account issues of public transport, access to services and infrastructure, and 'ghettoisation'. As they explain further, 'There are very few jobs on the urban fringe, a consequence of constructing residential communities with little space for anything else' (p. 238). Indeed, the consequences of this spatial shift to the urban fringe, they argue, are the increasing segregation of inequality. This is sometimes discussed as 'postcode inequality', where, as we alluded to above and in Chapter 1, measurable differences in equity, health, access to services and measures of social justice can be seen from postcode to postcode (Healey, 2019; Swan, 2005).

While there are significant issues and concerns for communities in the outer suburbs, there is also significant opportunity for engagement and for acknowledging and celebrating the social and cultural diversity of these neighbourhoods. As Warr and Robson (2013) write:

> Much stands to be gained from recognising that suburban hinterlands are also social frontiers in that they are sites of significant social changes that require innovative and creative approaches for fostering sociable and safe neighbourhoods. (p. 990)

Recognising the creative and cultural potential of these geographic sites also means acknowledging and addressing the stigma experienced by communities living in neighbourhoods or postcodes that are considered poorer or marginal. In turn, literature on place-based stigma points to the subversive potential of creative practices that can attend to these complex class relations. As Warr, Taylor and Jacobs argue, artistic practices can play a role in helping to understand, navigate and potentially challenge neighbourhood stigma, particularly when developed in partnership with affected communities through co-creation (2021).

Art and Cultural Citizenship in the City Fringe

In the context of this socio-spatial understanding of cities, ASEs have a potential role to play in connecting young people living in the urban fringe with artistic skills and interests to broader social and cultural networks, while also enabling them to understand the specific qualities of their own 'place'. Creative practice, particularly in the fields of music, dance and performance, offers a vehicle to explore the complexity of identity and culture—in terms of both individual experiences and the collective experiences that relate to belonging to a particular place marked by socio-economic conditions that tend to limit social capital. What is unique to these more performative art forms is that they revolve around the artists' 'voice'—spoken work, music, rap, dance and theatre are all creatively informed by individual expression and, in particular, vocalisation—especially storytelling. They also connect more directly to audiences. The less technologically mediated presence of live performance can enable opportunities for directly felt communication and exchange, while the affective reach of performance can be quite profound.

It is for these reasons that performing arts practices are often seen as effective in developing capacity for social and political critique and engendering more democratic forms of 'cultural citizenship' (Dickens & Lonie, 2013) or 'sociopolitical consciousness' (Ngo et al., 2017.). In a review of literature around performing arts practice and youth empowerment, for example, Ngo, Lewis and Maloney observed the specific qualities of creative production, writing 'Notably, the development of sociopolitical consciousness in the research we reviewed was entwined with the process of creating something with materials and people and structured to include various publics' (Ngo et al., 2017, p. 374). Anna

6 Creative Practice, Cultural Citizenship and the Urban Fringe 113

Hickey-Moody (2016), meanwhile, has theorised the political potential of youth arts through the concept of 'little publics', acknowledging the social, cultural and spatial specificity of each community of artists, and also their audience. Across the literature, it is clear that through performing their art, young artists can express their individual experiences in ways that connect to the specific social, economic and cultural conditions of their social and spatial place—with opportunities to build collective understandings of social and political issues. Indeed, through voicing their perspectives, young artists can, at times, offer forms of resistance and critique as well as model counter-hegemonic practices (Duncombe, 2007).

The flipside of this critical potential, however, is an equal risk of young people 'performing' their identity in ways that reinforce—rather than challenge—existing social conditions and stereotypes. As Nick Couldry writes in *Why Voice Matters: Culture and Politics After Neoliberalism* (2010):

> If, through an unequal distribution of narrative resources, the materials from which some people must build their account of themselves are not theirs to adapt or control, then this represents a deep denial of voice, a deep form of oppression. This is the oppression W. B. Dubois described as "double consciousness", a "sense of always looking at oneself through the eyes of others." (p. 9)

In Chapter 5, we discussed the ways that funders, for example, expect narratives of individual transformation (framed through a lens of overcoming hardship) to support their investment in community arts programs. The focus on individual storytelling and individual examples of 'overcoming' or 'success', that can be easily projected in youth community performing arts programs, align well with these more neoliberal interests.

This was evident for example in Luke Dickens and Douglas Lonie's study of young people developing lyrical expression in rap music at Ustudios, an arts venture established on the urban fringe of Brighton in the UK (2013). The authors describe a common pattern of young people describing their personal stories as a journey from hardship to success:

> Especially common was a sense of their past selves being 'trouble makers' and how their present selves had been able to 'move on', articulating an appreciation of the fact that while their own difficult circumstances might be out of their control, their lyrical practices could serve as a means for coping in moments when thoughts and feelings became difficult or distressing. (p. 67)

These stories of transformation and success, while positive in and of themselves, can deflect from the structural issues that give rise to socioeconomic disadvantage in the first place and, as discussed in Chapters 2 and 3, can also deflect audiences away from actively 'listening' to the issues that young people raise (Dreher, 2012).

These considerations are paramount in Elyse Gordon's analysis of youth empowerment programs in the USA, which we discussed briefly in Chapter 5. Gordon (2013) describes how an interest in success stories, particularly from funders, produces an aversion to working with young people who do not show the capacity for transformation or success—what she describes as the 'undeserving' youth, who are often either not included in these programs, or whose failure to succeed is structurally ignored. In relation to her case study organisation Youth Grow, for example, she writes:

> In the first instance, those youth deemed undeserving fail to receive any of the skills Youth Grow attempts to provide. The most vulnerable youth are the ones that lose. In the second instance, residual poverty knowledge blames individuals for their own poverty, warranting individual level solutions. This type of poverty governance cannot and will not ever address the structural barriers facing low-income urban youth. (p. 114)

Many ASEs operating in the performing arts can therefore struggle to find a balance between a focus on individual empowerment, on the one hand, and collective action or structural change, on the other.

Young artists telling their stories of personal overcoming is not inherently problematic, however, and in fact, these forms of personal expression have been shown to help young people mediate their complex social conditions, build literacy skills, gain confidence and access 'supportive modes of participation, inclusion and cultural citizenship' (Dickens &

Lonie, 2013, p. 60; Meade & Shaw, 2011). Questions then turn to *how* individual artists' stories are told, involving a recognition of the need to ask how their stories might be used by the community arts organisations or ASEs that they are involved with, how the young people involved might be framing their stories to conform to social/cultural expectations, how much freedom young artists have to create their own authentic narratives, and how these narratives might change over time?

When working collectively in arts projects, as opposed to individually, evidence shows that young people have further opportunities to navigate their personal position and its relation to broader social inequities. This was evident, for example, in Spiegel and Parent's (2018) study of youth circus programs in Canada, where the researchers identified this key tension between individualised transformation and collective political engagement. It was in the collaborations between young people that Spiegel and Parent saw potential for social change. They write:

> Those whose own individual and collective perspectives have been marginalized are able to creatively work together, affecting horizons of individual and collective futures. It is through such collective creative embodiment of alternative ways of engaging that such programmes may contribute to "micropolitical revolutions", providing tools for redressing the social inequities that dominate in contemporary urban centres. (p. 614)

To what extent, then, are ASEs able to address structural change and activate young peoples' political consciousness, or as Stephen Duncombe argues, to 'move cultural resistance into community development' (2007, p. 499)? What are the structural barriers to participation for young people living on the urban fringe? We turn to this question now as we conclude the chapter.

Show Me the Money: Art and Entrepreneurship in Outer Urban ASEs

For ASEs operating in the urban fringe, then, an understanding of the economic realities facing young people in their local neighbourhoods, and strategies to address barriers to educational, cultural and civic engagement, is crucial. For many young people experiencing financial hardship, engaging in 'art for art's sake' (Morgan, 2013) is less appealing—or, indeed, possible—than engaging in art with more practical and economic outcomes, including pathways to employment. We saw this in our interviews, observations and collaborations (workshops and exhibition) with young people from migrant and refugee backgrounds in Chapters 4 and 5, where we also drew on the work of various scholars in emphasising this point (Morgan & Idriss, 2012; Oppedal et al., 2017). A key feature of ASEs in this context, then, is providing the opportunity for paid work or, at the very least, facilitating the development of networks that can support work opportunities. This includes providing connections into the professional arts industry and enabling the development of entrepreneurial skills that can support careers in the creative industries.

These interventions explicitly recognise that artistic practices—when linked with entrepreneurship or opportunities for work—enable the development of broader networks beyond a specific locale, and therefore allow access to new opportunities, including career development and greater connection to the cultural life of the city (Hampshire & Matthijsse, 2010). Access to dominant or mainstream cultural sites and discourses is not necessarily transformative in itself—in fact, it can reinforce structures of inequality—but being active producers of culture, for example by performing original works for various publics, can, as we have previously noted, activate counter-hegemonic positions (Duncombe, 2007; Mouffe, 2013). This is to return to the idea of accessing 'bridging networks' beyond a particular geographic location. As Deborah Warr argues, such bridging can enable the development of social capital, particularly for communities living in areas of socio-economic disadvantage (2006). Warr writes, 'In contexts of disadvantage,

6 Creative Practice, Cultural Citizenship and the Urban Fringe 117

networks that provide bridges to new information and ideas heighten potential for 'getting ahead' and can be sources of social capital' (p. 503).

ASEs routinely work to provide bridges by linking the often young artists engaged with them to networks of professional creatives and industry; enabling those young people to present their work to diverse geographic and social audiences; and opening them up to opportunities that may not have been available otherwise. Equally, young creatives from the urban fringe (or experiencing other forces of marginalisation) are often drawn to ASEs for the opportunity to pursue professional art-making opportunities. Access to professional work experience was a key motivator, for example, for the young rap artists engaged at Ustudios, discussed earlier in the chapter. Dickens and Lonie found that treating young artists as professional musicians was key to engaging them (2013). They described the particular influence of a facilitator in the organisation, Max, who encouraged the emerging artists to record professionally:

> Thus, by focussing project activities around what the young people on the project had decided they wanted to do specifically, building vocal, compositional and other musical skills, and recording professional quality outputs, the project followed both the intrinsic means and instrumental ends of the participants themselves, rather than those of the adult stakeholders and agencies involved. (p. 64)

This focus on professionalisation speaks to another potential role of ASEs: addressing key gaps in conventional, and often traditionalist, arts education that tends to under emphasise the need for a knowledge of employability and entrepreneurship. As we have discussed in previous chapters, the precarious and ad hoc nature of the creative industries means that emerging artists need to develop a range of skills to participate and potentially thrive in these industries, including the ability to network, advocate for reasonable pay, manage multiple contracts and oversee finances. Ruth Bridgstock (2013) describes the importance of these skills, even for artists who are not profit-motivated:

> Juggling and blending multiple entrepreneurial bottom lines is central to arts entrepreneurship and to building sustainable arts careers [...] The ability to tap into and pursue personal career goals, while also being able to chase other shorter-term venture creation, project and enterprise goals successfully, involves both career identity depth and career identity adaptability on the part of the artist. (p. 130)

With their emphasis on *learning* alongside actually *creating and delivering* artistic production to audiences and publics, ASEs provide a natural context for these entrepreneurial skills. The life of an ASE is one that works on a continuum, from working to secure 'gigs' and exhibitions, managing multiple contracts, seeking funds from multiple sources (including grants and earned income), balancing values of economic sustainability alongside social and artistic goals, and simply trying to survive in complex market conditions (McQuilten et al., 2020).

As we have emphasised in this chapter, a push–pull between entrepreneurialism and community justice or 'cultural citizenship' features as a key tension for ASEs working with young people, including those living in the urban fringe. We move now to further explore this tension in Chapter 7, where we examine how these dual motives of professionalisation and social justice operate within our case study organisation, Outer Urban Projects (OUP). OUP is a performing arts company that works with young people on the urban fringe of Melbourne. Understanding the lived experience of young people engaging with the programs at OUP reveals both the precarity and opportunity of the creative industries, the potential for sociopolitical activation for young people living in 'poorer postcodes' and the interplay between individual aspirations and collective social change. We consider the ways in which young people working within the context of OUP are simultaneously pursuing their own individual careers in the performing arts, while harbouring aspirations to set up their own types of community-oriented and social ventures, with an interest in 'giving back' to community and thereby activating structural change.

References

Bridgstock, R. (2013). Not a dirty word: Arts entrepreneurship and higher education. *Arts and Humanities in Higher Education, 12*(2–3), 122–137.

Couldry, N. (2010). *Why voice matters: Culture and politics after neoliberalism.* Sage.

Dickens, L., & Lonie, D. (2013). Rap, rhythm and recognition: Lyrical practices and the politics of voice on a community music project for young people experiencing challenging circumstances. *Emotion, Space and Society, 9*, 59–71.

Dreher, T. (2012). A partial promise of voice: Digital storytelling and the limits of listening. *Media International Australia Incorporating Culture & Policy, 142*, 157–166.

Duncombe, S. (2007). (From) Cultural resistance to community development. *Community Development Journal, 42*(4), 490–500.

Eckardt, F. (2021). *Gentrification: Research and policy on urban displacement processes* (1st ed. 2021). Springer Fachmedien Wiesbaden.

Gordon, E. (2013). Under-served and un-deserving: Youth empowerment programs, poverty discourses and subject formation. *Geoforum, 50*, 107–116.

Hampshire, K., & Matthijsse, M. (2010). Can arts projects improve young people's wellbeing? A social capital approach. *Social Science & Medicine (1982), 71*(4), 708–716.

Harris, A. (2012). Art and gentrification: Pursuing the urban pastoral in Hoxton, London. *Transactions of the Institute of British Geographers, 37*(2), 226–241.

Healey, J. (2019). *Poverty and inequality in Australia.* The Spinney Press.

Hickey-Moody, A. (2016). Youth agency and adult influence: A critical revision of little publics. *The Review of Education/pedagogy/cultural Studies, 38*(1), 58–72.

Lindner, C., & Sandoval, G. (Eds). (2021). *Aesthetics of gentrification: Seductive spaces and exclusive communities in the neoliberal city.* Amsterdam University Press.

Martin, S., & Goodman, R. (2016). Living on the edge: New forms of poverty and disadvantage on the urban fringe. In C. Williams (Ed.), *Social work and the city: Urban themes in 21st century social work.* Palgrave Macmillan.

McQuilten, G., Warr, D., Humphery, K., & Spiers, A. (2020). Ambivalent entrepreneurs: Arts-based social enterprise in a neoliberal world. *Social Enterprise Journal, 16*(2), 121–140.

Meade, R., & Shaw, M. (2011). Community development and the arts: Sustaining the democratic imagination in lean and mean times. *Journal of Arts and Communities, 2*(1), 65–80.

Morgan, G., & Idriss, S. (2012). "Corsages on their parents' jackets": Employment and aspiration among Arabic-speaking youth in Western Sydney. *Journal of Youth Studies, 15*(7), 929–943.

Morgan, H. (2013). Art for art's sake. *Grove Art Online.* Accessed 24 January 2022, https://www.oxfordartonline.com/groveart/view/10.1093/gao/9781884446054.001.0001/oao-9781884446054-e-7000004365

Mouffe, C. (2013). *Agonistics: Thinking the world politically.* Verso.

Tunalı, T. (2021). *Art and gentrification in the changing neoliberal landscape.* Taylor & Francis Group.

Ngo, B., Lewis, C., & Maloney Leaf, B. (2017). Fostering sociopolitical consciousness with minoritized youth: Insights from community-based arts programs. *Review of Research in Education, 41*(1), 358–380.

Oppedal, B., Guribye, E., & Kroger, J. (2017). Vocational identity development among unaccompanied refugee minors. *International Journal of Intercultural Relations, 60*, 145–159.

Rich, M. A. (2019). "Artists are a tool for gentrification": Maintaining artists and creative production in arts districts. *International Journal of Cultural Policy, 25*(6), 727–742.

Spiegel, J. B., & Parent, S. N. (2018). Re-approaching community development through the arts: A "critical mixed methods" study of social circus in Quebec. *Community Development Journal, 53*(4), 600–617.

Swan, W. (2005). *Postcode: The splintering of a nation.* Pluto Press.

Warr, D. (2006). Gender, class, and the art and craft of social capital. *Sociological Quarterly, 47*(3), 497–520.

Warr, D., & Robson, B. (2013). "Everybody's different": Struggles to find community on the suburban frontier. *Housing Studies, 28*(7), 971–992.

Warr, D., Taylor, G., & Jacobs, K. (2021). You can't eat art! But can arts-based research challenge neighbourhood stigma? *Qualitative Research, 21*(2), 268–287.

7

Outer Urban Projects: Community Building Versus Mainstreaming

Abstract Outer Urban Projects (OUP) is a performing arts based social organisation, with a social enterprise arm, that operates in the outer northern suburbs of Melbourne, Australia. OUP targets diverse, socio-economically disadvantaged communities, and takes the starting point of a professional performing arts company to engage young people in a range of short and long term creative programs across artforms including dance, rap, music, song and theatre. At OUP, professionalism is a key strategy for engaging young people in arts activity: not only does it validate an emerging artists' capacity for creative expression and the cultural contribution of their individual 'voice', it also supports the immediate needs of young people, particularly those from lower socio-economic backgrounds, to generate income and find meaningful work. This positioning also helps to shift perceptions away from deficit-based understandings of the social reality of living in the outer urban fringe, and to emphasise instead the strengths of emerging artists in the city's outer suburbs. While the broader goal of OUP is to develop a new generation of professional artists and support them to access opportunities in the industry, many OUP participants and alumni are conflicted in their goals of achieving personal success, on the one hand, and 'giving back' to their immediate communities, on the other. This chapter explores two key questions about the role of ASEs in generating social change: does a focus on individual stories of success come at the cost of advocating for structural change in the educational and work opportunities afforded to young people living on the margins? And are OUP alumni reproducing a model of community arts development that they have learned from OUP, rather than transitioning into the so called 'mainstream'?

Keywords Outer urban projects · Gentrification · Urban fringe · Performing arts · Transformation · Young creatives · Art · Social enterprise · Employment

Introduction

It is a Saturday afternoon in Broadmeadows, a suburb on the fringe of Melbourne's outer north, June 2019. The atmosphere in the auditorium is full of heightened emotions, big, ascendent, harmonised vocals fill the air along with the rapid tapping beat of hands drumming the tabla, people swaying and dancing to the music, all affected, smiling and clapping along. This is the Hume Studios dance and music theatre community showcase, and it is indicative of how Outer Urban Projects (OUP) works with diverse performing artists in a way that aims to 'create quality performing art, employment and social engagement for and with young people in Melbourne's outer north' (OUP, 2022b). Over two afternoons, Hume Studios presents a spirited showcase of dancers, musicians and vocalists highlighting what the promotional material touts as 'the best of Hume's mighty arsenal of emerging talent', blending a hybrid of genres that includes Islander culture, hip hop, spoken word, a string orchestra and Middle Eastern drummers (OUP, 2022c). Lively performances are punctuated with moments of testimony, where OUP's ensemble of talent express passionately the transformation they have experienced during their time with the company and how dance and music is integral to their lives. This is evident also in the promotional trailer for Hume Studios, where singer Melaia Vugona Sadranu proclaims that participating 'feels like hope', and dancer Damian Seddon enthuses that 'hip hop can spread emotions'. Eugene Osei, shown backstage in the

7 Outer Urban Projects: Community Building Versus Mainstreaming

same trailer, continues this theme by stating 'when I dance I'm so happy', the trailer then cuts to a scene of charismatic tabla drummer Joseph Samarani on stage rousing an audience by declaring 'I love music so much' (OUP, 2022d). The young performers from OUP that we interviewed for this study, and whose words fill this chapter, have continually testified to these transformative and empowering facets of performing with the company. Nadine, for example, asserted 'So coming to Outer Urban Projects and the stuff that they do, I love it to be honest. I love how empowering it is. When they do shows there's always a meaning behind it. There's always something that has to be said'.

OUP is a performing arts-based social organisation (with a social enterprise arm) operating in the outer northern suburbs of Melbourne that targets diverse, socio-economically disadvantaged communities. OUP takes the starting point of a professional performing arts company to engage young people in a range of short- and long-term creative programs across art forms including dance, rap, music, song and theatre. The organisation has worked hard to position itself as a serious arts company and collaborates with esteemed artists, directors, producers and choreographers to build this profile and position. This emphasis was evident when Kate Gillick, Executive Producer, gave an overview of the organisation:

> We're a very artist driven company – that's kind of our history ... people want to come into the weekly tutorials and just engage with the performing arts, or be exposed to it, come in and do their thing and just feel good about themselves, they can do that! ... We find such a hunger for performance from our guys, you know, they're demanding from us all the time – we can't keep up sometimes. When's the next gig?

As discussed in Chapter 6, professionalism is a powerful strategy for engaging young people in arts activity: not only does it validate an emerging artists' capacity for creative expression and the cultural contribution of their individual 'voice', it also supports the immediate needs of young people, particularly those from lower socio-economic backgrounds, to generate income and find meaningful work (Dickens & Lonie, 2013). For OUP, this positioning also helps to shift perceptions

Fig. 7.1 A promotional image for Hume Studios (Image courtesy of Outer Urban Projects)

away from deficit-based understandings of the social reality of living in the outer urban fringe and to emphasise instead the strengths of emerging artists in the city's outer suburbs (Fig. 7.1). While the broader goal of OUP is to develop a new generation of professional artists and support them to access opportunities in the industry, many OUP participants and alumni are conflicted in their goals of achieving personal success, on the one hand, and 'giving back' to their immediate communities, on the other. This raises key questions for an understanding of the role of ASEs in generating social change (ones that we have already begun to explore in the previous two case studies): does a focus on individual stories of success come at the cost of advocating for structural change in the educational and work opportunities afforded to young people living on the margins? And are OUP alumni reproducing a model of community arts development that they have learned from OUP, rather than transitioning into the so-called mainstream? These questions inform the discussion that follows.

Performing the North

Melbourne's outer north represents a defined geographical region covering four key municipal areas: Moreland, Darebin, Hume and Whittlesea. These areas are experiencing fast population growth and encompass a vibrant mix of new and established residential areas, major industrial and commercial precincts and vast expanses of urban parkland and rural fringe areas. Like many suburbs located on the outer edges of a large metropolitan city, this relatively socio-economically disadvantaged community experiences a lack of access to infrastructure, including resources to foster culture and the arts, particularly the performing arts (Parliament of Victoria, 2013; Watts, 2013). OUP is one of the few arts organisations in the outer north and it is a key goal of the organisation to address these issues of access and opportunity.

OUP introduces their students to rather unique creative opportunities that often mix genres and styles in contemporary, large-scale performances and opens up possibilities for artists lacking experience and access to mainstream arts and culture. As emerging artist Daniel explained:

> I'm trying to get some gigs for myself and in Outer Urban you can do that. Like in October we've got this orchestra thing happening. It's a big thing and it's the first opportunity for me to play with the Melbourne Symphony Orchestra [...] And lute too, they want me to play the lute. You know it's an orchestra. I mean a band okay, but orchestra? This is a big exciting thing, you know.

From their base in Coburg North, in a mixed-used creative site that they share with a youth mental health service called Orygen, OUP tackles issues of inequality in the arts industry by providing emerging artists with access to a generative and creative environment shaped by skilled mentors, trainers and artists. They focus on engaging a local community of young people with aspirations to develop creative and performance skills, and their families, schools and associated community organisations. While they don't define or name specific kinds of marginalisation or access barriers as a requirement for young people to participate in their programs, OUP works with a large number of culturally diverse young people including young people from First Nations backgrounds from Australia and elsewhere. Careful not to overplay the specifics of marginalisation, OUP's outward facing communications do nevertheless speak directly to the issues of socio-economic disadvantage of the outer northern suburbs in which they work. For example, on their website, OUP states their aim is to 'give voice to the unexpressed aspirations and creative potential of ghettoised, culturally diverse emerging artists whose origins span five continents' (OUP, 2022a). In this way, they shift focus away from individual disadvantage or marginality (defined, for example, by a young artist's cultural identity, housing status or mental health issues), and instead work with the structural inequalities generated by rapid urban development and gentrification in a broader sense—especially what they describe as 'ghettoisation'.

A key focus therefore for OUP is providing links and bridges (in spatial terms) between the cultural lives of young people living in the outer north of Melbourne with the opportunities and cultural life of the inner city, such as Melbourne's central CBD 'Arts Precinct'. They do this through staging events and collaborations with leading arts venues such as the Arts Centre (a prestigious Melbourne venue that hosts major arts productions and is home to some of the largest stages in Australia) and with respected companies such as Chunky Move (a bold contemporary dance company that showcases Australian dance talent) and La Mama Theatre (a more boutique inner city theatre that showcases independent, high-quality 'art-house' productions). Additionally, OUP performers are introduced to professionals in the creative arts who work across industries and geographic locations. OUP thus works to produce a mix of large-scale, high-quality productions involving well-known artists, writers and performers with community-focused events showcasing diverse new talent (from percussion and vocal performance to hip hop dance and spoken word). By this means, OUP provides professional development, training and employment pathways for young artists.

A social justice approach informs the aims and goals of the organisation, complemented by staff who share lived experience of growing

7 Outer Urban Projects: Community Building Versus Mainstreaming

up and living in the outer suburbs—one staff member, for example, attended Reservoir High School, one of OUP's key referral partners—and this filters into its social enterprise activity, which operates as a kind of performing arts agency that 'hires out' artists for performances. The social enterprise arm of OUP produces supplementary income to the mainstay of grants and philanthropic funding. It also provides paid work to their artists along with networking opportunities. This hybrid business model, which combines self-generated revenue from ticket sales and social enterprise activity with major arts funding from government bodies such as the Australia Council for the Arts alongside project-based philanthropic grants, enables OUP to avoid over-reliance on any single source of income. The flipside of this hybridity is the complex task of relationship management with a wide array of funders, arts partners and community organisations, and the equally complex challenge of delivering different kinds of performance events across the arts, corporate and community sectors. As Kate told us, 'We're working in this very different terrain across sectors: youth sector, arts sector, venues […] we work with a lot of people across a lot of different contexts in order to create this'.

Young people engaged with OUP tend to have links to a range of other social and educational services and are most often introduced to OUP through their schools via after-school dance and music programs. This wider ecology is important, as staff member Cameron elucidated:

> A lot of our community might be going to health organisations. Or to other educational institutions, or to their school for support. In that situation we would be getting information or advice about how the community is responding to certain issues. There can be a circle of knowledge that's shared between community and this organisation.

After participating in workshops, young creatives showing potential are encouraged to participate in further programs and professional development opportunities, leading, for example, to participation in major arts productions. In addition to paid performing jobs or 'gigs' through the social enterprise arm, OUP artists also have the opportunity to work as teachers and mentors in the OUP community if they show a greater commitment and longer-term engagement with the organisation. Significant career opportunities have been obtained by emerging artists working with OUP including working on major OUP productions such as Vessel (2017) and Grand DiVisions (2015) at the Arts Centre. Emerging performing artist Jacob spoke about how he has obtained teaching through OUP as well as connections to producers for big performances:

> With Outer Urban, they also got me a gig, a crazy gig, at the Arts Centre. I've been in two shows. One was Vessel, and that was their own project —I loved that one. But the even better one was Lord of the Flies. That involved contemporary [English choreographer] Matthew Bourne. They hosted one of the workshop auditions. I was like, you know what? I'm going to try it. I went through three phases then yes, got in, and so cool. I got to be on [the television show] The Project. That was really unreal.

The flipside of this artistic development model—which starts with casual engagement after school and progresses to more professionalisation—is that it tends to favour young people with higher levels of 'talent' and motivation. This is a common feature of youth empowerment programs, as we discussed in Chapter 6 in relation to Elyse Gordon's analysis of youth community organisation, Youth Grow (Gordon, 2013). OUP tries to mitigate this by providing wrap-around support for young people who, for example, may lack the support of their families to engage in arts programs, or who may be less motivated due to the competing demands of school, work and family and community responsibilities. OUP acknowledges that while their programs and events demonstrate the skills of emerging artists, there is a risk that other talented community members may miss out on opportunities. The OUP Crisis Fund, for example, was developed to offer fast response support and assistance to emerging artists by addressing individual financial, housing or other complex needs. As staff member Mitch explained:

> We've actually got what we call a crisis fund which was money that we fundraised for […] This is a company of artists and we believe in the social impact of art but there is a limit to that. Some of our kids needed support in moments of crisis. We had a young man who was on a type

of temporary protection visa – he was a boat arrival – and we supported some legal costs. We've got another young man who had insecure accommodation so we were able to pay for some emergency accommodation for a while.

As Wright, John, Aleggia and Sheel write in their evaluation of a national community arts program for Canadian youth from low-income communities, parental support and cultural connection to creativity can be a key factor in engaging and not engaging young people in the arts (Wright et al., 2006). While some OUP artists describe having the support of their families—and this is often due to relatives also having creative backgrounds or interests—others talk about how OUP 'opened up their (family's) minds' to creative careers and that their parents became more open to them being creative professionals after seeing them perform at paid shows. This was evident, for example, when artist Nadine told us about her family:

> Our parents didn't really see the career sense until we got more involved with Outer Urban Projects […] If we were going to go into the police force or something we would probably get more support in doing that than doing something like this, the creative arts […] OUP is sort of opening up the family's eyes to support their kids in this. My family's probably a good testament of that.

These experiences of young people involved in OUP, talking through the complexities of pursuing a career in the arts from a context where these pathways are not obvious or well-supported, speak to the social dynamics of growing up and living in an outer urban community. The next part of this chapter will look in more detail at how OUP is providing 'bridging networks' to connect young artists with spatial and economic bridges into the arts industry (Warr, 2006).

'Bridging Networks'—Pathways into the Arts Industry

As discussed above, OUP introduces their emerging artists to the arts industry in Melbourne, enabling opportunities for access to professional development and work opportunities that are difficult to otherwise access due to geographic and socio-economic barriers. This sense of connection to industry is important to the young artists involved. As Diyala described:

> I just remember being so excited, because they give us a call sheet [a performance schedule for cast and crew] and it says how long we are there for and what we need to do and the payment. Yeah, everyone was excited about that, because it made us feel like we were professionals.

The emphasis at OUP on connecting to the wider arts industry speaks to the importance of social capital—the ability to build social relationships and networks across class divides—and to develop bridges between neighbourhoods and postcodes. Kate explained:

> As an arts company we try and work in ways where we're always connecting. It's not an insular thing where we just work within our beat [...] It's about our community getting exposure to that (inner city arts) precinct, and what it offers. Those things don't exist within a certain radius of where our community lives.

As discussed in Chapters 2 and 6, Deborah Warr (2006) talks about the importance of both 'bonding networks' (relational links between family and friends) and 'bridging networks' (links to people, networks and opportunities outside of a community) in supporting people to develop social capital. OUP has elements of both bonding and bridging networks. The close relationships between staff and peers at OUP enable social inclusion, what might be considered a 'safe space' to explore questions of identity and place, and a sense of shared belonging (Roestone Collective, 2014). However, the connections that OUP provides to professional artists and arts organisations, and participation in a wide range of public and private events through its social enterprise, mean that artists are experiencing new ideas, places and people. Emerging artists at OUP describe being introduced to lots of new, like-minded creative people that inspire them and who they are eager to collaborate with. Jacob, for example, described his relationship with OUP peers as 'better friendships' than the ones he had prior to OUP: they are helpful 'contacts' for the future. Some artists, such as Matilda, spoke of becoming aware that they are interested in 'networking' and developing new 'collaborations'. OUP thus creates an environment where participants can build trust with each other over time and create bonds that lead to new opportunities.

In spatial terms, OUP provides its young artists with links between their immediate community/ies in the outer north of Melbourne and a broader (inner urban) cultural landscape—with potential cross-pollination between different place/s and social networks. Participating in this broader arts landscape allows the young performers at OUP to discover, and open up to, new experiences and worldviews. Indeed, some of the young artists we interviewed noted that as a result of participating in OUP, they have discovered a new sense of independence, become more engaged with the broader cultural activity of Melbourne and been introduced to new art forms and aesthetic experiences. Artist Jacob spoke to this when he told us about how his personal interests have evolved since being involved with OUP (Fig. 7.2):

> My interests have changed. I used to be just into the shopping centres, the movies, but now I love going to forests, I like going for drives out to the beach and I love going to galleries. I love going to the Arts Centre. I just love doing things like that. It's just fun. I get joy out of it.

Another important function of bridging networks is the development of entrepreneurial skills—the ability to self-promote, obtain new work and gain access to larger platforms for performing, from festivals to arts companies. OUP is quite direct in trying to foster this entrepreneurialism in their emerging artists. Through OUP, artists describe being exposed to, and viewing, a way of working that inspires them. They are taught how to submit invoices, get gigs, devise their own work and present

Fig. 7.2 Artist Ruci Kaisila performing at Hume Studios (Image courtesy of Outer Urban Projects)

themselves as professionals. Jacob noted, for example, how OUP pushed him to 'do better for yourself' and worked to 'clean you up, polish you up'. He explained how he has learnt to 'self-manage' and that OUP taught him how to 'build myself up on my own'. Some of the young artists at OUP thus talked of starting their own bands and companies, or wanting to develop their own shows, precisely because of increased self-efficacy and self-esteem. Notably, many of the young artists involved with OUP demonstrated that they have become comfortable and literate in the 'gigging economy' of the creative labourer, and have taken on board the entrepreneurial, self-branding spirit that is necessary to secure work in the performing arts (Bridgstock, 2013).

Accompanying their new ease at presenting themselves as creative professionals, OUP's emerging artists often speak of being busy or hectic as they juggle day jobs, study and meet the demands of gigs or teaching with OUP. They experience the after-hours, irregular and precarious nature of their creative, project-based work. As Matilda commented, 'The hardest thing would probably be this year, because now that I'm studying it's hard to juggle work – like, doing their gigs and also study'. Like many creative professionals, OUP artists are aware that it is useful to be supported by a more stable day job to compliment the irregular nature of gigs, but this often means their lives become 'jam packed'. Fetu talked about the importance of teaching work at OUP, to provide a more regular income and complement the irregularity of performances:

> The gigs are good but no, they're good for a limited time but as in ongoing work, as in like tutoring – which is why it's awesome that OUP have got the tutoring, those sorts of programs – but that could haven't been done if people hadn't gone to gigs in the first place.

Here, it becomes clear that there is a reciprocal relationship between doing gigs, or more sporadic performances which build profile and professional networks, and the opportunity for finding and securing more regular paid work. In their study of artists' incomes in Australia, cultural economists David Throsby and Katya Petetskaya observed this tendency for artists to develop parallel income streams, often in other industries, to support their practice (Throsby & Petetskaya, 2017).

Treating young people as professional artists therefore achieves multiple goals for OUP, and this echoes the findings of Dickens and Lonie's study of *Ustudios* in the outer suburbs of Brighton, UK, (discussed in Chapter 6), where studio mentor Max emphasised the importance of taking music seriously and providing professional recording opportunities (Dickens & Lonie, 2013). For OUP, the benefits of this approach include attracting young artists with existing talents and potential to develop careers in the arts, and also engaging young people from the outer suburbs who are attracted to opportunities for income generation through their creative passions, as opposed to the more traditionalist pursuit of art for art's sake. This is what Dickens and Lonie describe as meeting both the artistic and practical motivators of young people—and represents a shift in thinking in socially-engaged arts by resolving what they argue is a false dichotomy between instrumental or pragmatic artistic output (e.g. making money), on the one hand, and intrinsic, or a more purist view of creativity, on the other. As Ruth Bridgstock (2013) argues, the challenge of bringing together artistic vision with work opportunities is central to the way all artists function in contemporary markets. This negotiation of the creative and economic, Bridgstock argues, is not properly acknowledged by industry and is not well taught in art schools:

> The ability to tap into and pursue personal career goals, while also being able to chase other shorter-term venture creation, project and enterprise goals successfully, involves both career identity depth and career identity adaptability on the part of the artist. (2013, p. 130)

So what are the job opportunities and pathways for emerging artists at OUP? A key finding of our study of OUP is that many of their artists have simultaneous goals to pursue a career outside of, or adjacent to, the arts (e.g. in teaching, youth work or hairdressing), while pursuing ambitions to become professional performers, theatremakers, writers, actors or musicians. We note this trend, while also observing that OUP artists are notably aspirational, with many developing their creative practice for several years. Cody, for example, told us that he 'wants to become famous'. Jacob similarly spoke of a direct goal to achieve fame:

> I've got a bucket list for my dance career, where I want to hit. One, I want to own my own dance studio eventually [...] When I'm 25, that's my goal. I want to become an international choreographer. I'm kind of heading down that path already, which is good.

This speaks to OUP's approach of valuing professionalism and collaborating with industry professionals and well-known artists, producers and choreographers to situate the organisation and its artists as a highly regarded arts company within the industry. However, this is juggled with the parallel OUP emphasis on the youth arts and community development dimensions of their work.

The same kind of juggling of priorities is evident at the level of individual performers. Alongside their professional ambitions, many OUP artists talk about 'back up' careers that reveal a strong degree of ambivalence about the stability and viability of careers in the creative industries—and which also speak to the relative challenges of their situated experience. When the students discuss pursuing further education at TAFE or university, for example, it is often not in performing arts but in a more reliable, employable field such as social work, business or science (and we have seen a similar attitude evident in our two other case study organisations). Notwithstanding this, most OUP artists see these training courses and careers as supporting or complementing their creative pursuits. Many of them, for instance, want to teach dance or start dance companies that support young people in a similar way to OUP, so training in youth work, business or teaching are pragmatic options that help them pursue those aims. Matilda explained, 'I chose [to study] youth work because I know in the future it could help me run my dance workshops and stuff like that with young people'. Similarly, Diyala talked about undertaking a business course in order to open a dance studio in the future. Both are looking to use their teaching skills, gained at OUP, to provide more stable income while also pursuing individual dance careers.

Others, however, are working towards securing careers outside the arts, like Beth, who insisted 'I have an interest in science outside performing arts, so that's like my other route to what I want to do'. Similarly, Rosalie explained that she had chosen to pursue an apprenticeship in hairdressing, and that this was explicitly related to the precarity and challenges of trying to work in the creative industries:

> I used to want it to be like a pathway or a career, but I don't know. I didn't lose my passion for it, I just decided that, you know, it's very hard to get into that industry nowadays [...] So I decided that keeping it on the side is cool. If anything ever happens with it, like I've got it to back me up and stuff. But I don't know, I just think hairdressing would be the most successful out of both.

A critical awareness of the barriers to participating in the arts was also expressed by Daniel, who told us 'I love creating, I love being creative. It's a bit hard to do it on my own because I haven't got the resources or the power to do it on my own'. This awareness of the structural limitations of their situations, and a critical engagement with the realities of the creative industries, speaks to the ways in which OUP supports their artists to 'speak our mind' about issues that matter to them (Rosalie).

The challenges of building a career in the arts, articulated clearly by many OUP artists, speak to an important dimension of bridging networks. Being introduced to mainstream art and culture is not transformative in and of itself. As Katherine Hampshire and Mathilde Matthijsse (2010) argue, social capital bridging can potentially involve young people needing to 'buy into and express cultural tastes and values of the dominant group' which, in turn, can cause disconnections from local bonding networks (p. 713). OUP counteracts this risk of assimilation into dominant culture by encouraging their artists to embrace their own unique cultures, creative influences and individual approaches. A central aim of OUP is to enable their young artists to develop and present work on mainstream stages—creative works that they describe as 'hybrid, contemporary, traditional, culturally eclectic and clashing transnational experience of the outer urban belt' (OUP, 2016–2020). In the light of this challenging push–pull between bridging young people with the mainstream art industry and appreciating the creativity already present in their local contexts, a more pertinent question might then be: how are the emerging artists at OUP challenging, changing or shaping mainstream culture? We now turn to consider this dimension of OUP's work with young artists in the final section of the chapter.

Cultural Citizenship or the Paradox of 'Telling My Story'

One of the strengths of OUP's programs is that they give students the autonomy to develop original work, engage in a diversity of contemporary performing arts practices and mix genres and styles. Jacob described being enabled to 'go with your own style' and 'have your own fun', and notes that OUP is 'open to how I want to do it'. Others speak of enjoying classes that are free of assessment. It's not 'schoolwork': the focus is on exploring and sharing creativity. Performing, in and of itself, is both challenging and exhilarating—offering a great sense of achievement—and providing an escape from day-to-day realities. As Nadine articulated:

> Most of the times when we go through stuff – issues, when we come off the stage we just feel empowered. We're like, "That's nothing to us. If we can do this we can conquer whatever." That's the sort of feeling that we get after we'd performed and stuff but obviously just in terms of getting there it's such a struggle. Just get in on that stage and then afterwards you're just like, "Oh my, gosh." Especially when you're acknowledged from people that you don't even know and they just love – they're just accepting of who you are there.

The benefits of this platform for expression are multiple, with OUP artists often speaking during the interviews of greater confidence and wellbeing, having expanded opportunities, feeling accepted and doing what they love. Diyala summed this up well when talking about her experience being at OUP: 'What I've gained: guidance, growth, opportunities, experience, foundation and staying involved in something you like'.

In terms of the more specific question of how OUP might foster what Stephen Duncome refers to as 'cultural resistance' (2007), OUP provides a platform for their artists to develop both individual means of self-expression and collective understandings of their social, cultural and political environments. This is what Ngo, Lewis and Maloney describe as the development of sociopolitical consciousness: 'Speaking from one's own circumstance is the foundation for identifying collective injustices, constructing a critique of inequality, and developing agency to advance social change' (2017, p. 362). OUP therefore gives young artists opportunities to share their views on a range of issues and tell their own stories—which contribute to individual performances, but are also used in the creation and development of large productions. Nadine explained how working together to develop larger performances creates a bridge between individual and collective experience: 'You kind of hear everyone's voice in the piece [...] They just take you as you are and use that as a piece'.

These opportunities to have a voice provide a starting point for OUP artists to unpack questions of place and identity, and find ways to express concerns. As Nadine further described:

That's one thing that I'm so proud of being part of Outer Urban Projects. And that's why I've been here for so long [...] They give a voice to, I guess they say things that should be said that haven't been said.

The potential impacts of this development of voice, agency and cultural citizenship were particularly poignant when Diyala explained how she has used the skills from OUP to explore, unpack and share her personal experience as an Indigenous artist coming to terms with the impacts of Australia's colonial history. She commented:

I interpreted my Indigenous cultural background of the stolen generation into my dance piece and did a kind of contemporary based performance of that story, that history [...] I also did it at one of the NAIDOC[1] week events this year, and there were a lot of elders and everything, and community members there. Got a lot of feedback from them, about how it moved them and that there's more of those type of things that need to be shown through dance or music.

Research on youth development in the arts points to the importance of these opportunities for young people to share their perspectives and give voice to their experiences, both individual and collective. For Butterwick and Roy, the development of voice for people experiencing the impacts of marginalisation enables the generation of 'pluralistic democracy' (2016, p. 9), while Nick Couldry, who's work we have drawn on in previous chapters, connects the activation of voice with political potential, particularly in shifting subjectivities away from being reduced to market-value (2010).

Along with the benefits of personal storytelling, however, comes an equal risk that young people revert to stereotypical narratives of transformation, or self-identify with narratives of disadvantage. Rather than transforming subjectivities or changing mainstream narratives, in this case voice can be used to reinforce dominant tropes. Unequal power dynamics between young people sharing their experiences, and how their stories are used, might perpetuate problematic subjectivities or as

---

[1] NAIDOC is a week-long series of events, held annually in July in Australia, that celebrate the history, culture and achievements of Aboriginal and Torres Strait Islander peoples.

Couldry argues, 'undermine voice' (Couldry, 2010, p. 2). A number of the OUP student interviewees, without prompting, readily offered their stories of hardship prior to getting involved with OUP, or testified to the ways OUP has changed them for the better. For example, Jacob told us how performing took him:

> Out of that danger where I could've gone down that wrong pathway. I could've done all the bad choices. I could've got arrested more times. It really took me out of that position and really lightened me up, really opened me up to the world, and really got me down a pathway that I really wanted to do.

This doesn't reflect on OUP specifically, but rather, indicates that via life experience and engagement with services more generally, young people from the outer northern suburbs of Melbourne might be habituated to understanding themselves through a lens of disadvantage, notwithstanding the socio-economic reality of the marginality that may have experienced. The artists at OUP come from diverse backgrounds: some detail their difficulties at school, hanging with the 'wrong people', encountering trouble with the police or being in and out of care. For example, Cody explained that prior to getting involved in OUP, he would 'get up to mischief, smoking and drinking, wagging, stealing, not coming home on time, all of that, typical teenager. Family, annoying. Getting clustered, getting blamed for everything, no freedom'. Others described barriers encountered when living with a disability, experiences of bullying, financial hardship or arriving in Australia as a refugee.

For OUP, individual stories of transformation are crucial for the organisation to assess its impact and to share this impact with funders and stakeholders. As Kate argued:

> In the philanthropic sector you really have to repeat that language back to people in terms that fall within their funding: vulnerability, disadvantage, marginalisation and diversity, inclusion, all these things.

The challenge, however, is to negotiate between these examples of individual marginalisation and the potential for OUP artists to effect collective or structural change and to shift such discourses of marginality. OUP tries to address this problem in a number of ways. Firstly, as we have noted previously, OUP shifts their public image away from that of a community development organisation and towards the image of a professional performing arts company. This diverts public attention from their artists' relative socio-economic and spatial marginality and allows the organisation to focus more directly on their creative talents. Secondly, as discussed at the start of this chapter, OUP specifically avoids the language of marginalisation. Kate explained that the organisation often uses the term 'ghettoisation' to speak to the structural issues that artists living in the outer north of Melbourne face. She commented:

> When you're leaving people off the main stages, and when you're not investing in programs in areas [like the outer north], it's actually what you're doing, you're ghettoising people, you're pocketing them, and pushing them out.

A further significant way that OUP's young artists show their concern to drive structural—rather than personal—change is when they talk about the value of giving back to the local community. Many are inspired by OUP's model and wish to create their own youth-focused studios or companies. This came out, for example, when Nadine spoke to us about her future aspirations:

> The big end goal, I want to do sort of what OUP are doing with the community [...] I'd like to work a lot more with indigenous community here in Melbourne. Or even if I moved somewhere to Cairns or something. And go with sort of what they're doing here with the music. That's why I wanted to go into social work so I had more experience in working with families and then working with youth.

Interest in pursuing careers in teaching or youth work, as we have noted, is a pragmatic way that many OUP artists enact these values. It is significant that many of OUP's artists talk about their pathways and future in terms of these interests in teaching and working in community—in this sense, they are replicating the values and model of OUP in

7 Outer Urban Projects: Community Building Versus Mainstreaming 141

how they envisage their 'transitions', over and above more obvious goals to transition into 'mainstream' careers (Fig. 7.3).

Meanwhile, both the organisation and its artists are subject to, and trying to resist, the challenging forces of mainstream markets and urban development. OUP is constantly navigating these challenges in trying to secure funding and grow, to develop productive partnerships with the mainstream arts industry and within their community ecology of schools, local government and social services. This negotiation was a strong theme, for example, when the authors facilitated an 'organisational mapping' workshop with OUP staff to delve into the complex networks of relationships—community, industry and government—that staff navigate in operating the organisation and its social enterprise arm. When staff were asked to draw a representation of the organisation in

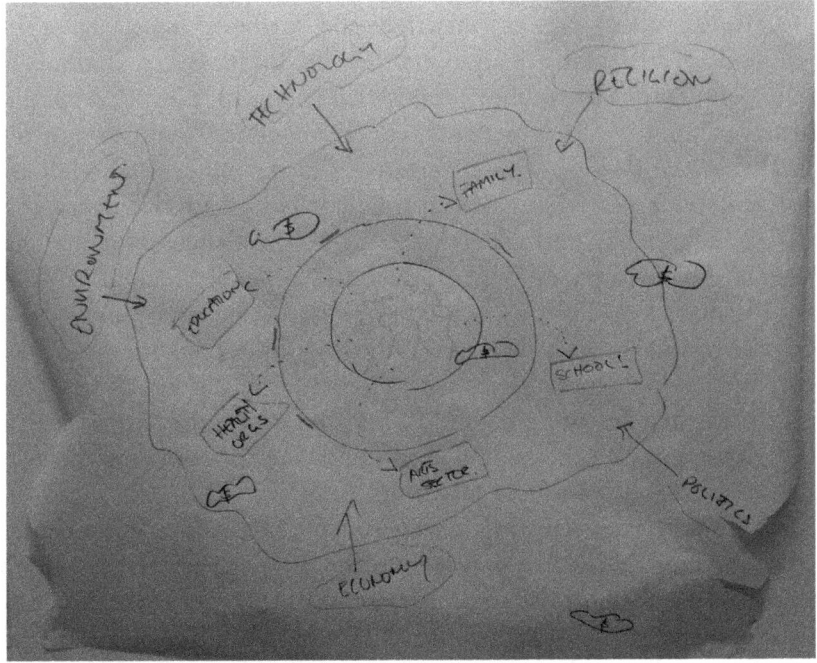

Fig. 7.3 Image developed in the OUP's organisational mapping workshop facilitated by the research team, August 2018

visual form, the resulting image (perhaps unsurprisingly) resembled an ecology—with community at the centre and networks revolving around this central community of artists. Interestingly, their map also featured a powerful external band that represented the external challenges and pressures that OUP, and their artists, work within. Cameron explained:

> This line just represents the fluidity of the external environment and pressure that bears on all of this. And that's all the way from religion to the environment, politics, the economy, and technology. And I feel like that impacts – or can have an impact on the organisation and also the community.

Conclusion

As an independent arts organisation and art-based social enterprise that works with young people on the urban fringe of Melbourne, OUP focuses on providing professional opportunities to emerging artists, enabling 'bridging networks' to advance social capital while also supporting the development of creative expression. It is through this creative development that young people involved in OUP activate their 'voices', individually and collectively, and reflect critically on the challenges of growing up and living in the outer north of Melbourne. As we have discovered, young people are bringing their concerns about issues of social inequality into dialogue with their aspirations for the future: firstly by developing a range of 'back up' careers to support the precarity of a creative arts life and secondly by aspiring to reproduce the values of OUP in supporting other young people and communities through access to creative arts programs and platforms.

To return to our opening questions, OUP treads a delicate path of encouraging individual aspirations for creative success within the context of challenging the structural constraints imposed by discourses of cultural and spatial marginality. While some young creatives at OUP choose to replicate the community-oriented values of OUP instead of aspiring to 'mainstream' transitions, these choices reflect a critical understanding of their social conditions and a desire to create positive structural change within their own communities. As we have discovered, this unexpected outcome of the ASE model at OUP is one that indicates the potential for young creatives to forge unique pathways in the creative industries, pathways that marry individual aspiration with values of community and collective social change.

References

Bridgstock, R. (2013). Not a dirty word: Arts entrepreneurship and higher education. *Arts and Humanities in Higher Education, 12*(2–3), 122–137.

Butterwick, S., & Roy, C. (Eds.). (2016). *Working the margins of community-based adult learning: The power of arts-making in finding voice and creating conditions for seeing/listening*. Sense Publishers.

Couldry, N. (2010). *Why voice matters: Culture and politics after neoliberalism*. Sage.

Dickens, L., & Lonie, D. (2013). Rap, rhythm and recognition: Lyrical practices and the politics of voice on a community music project for young people experiencing challenging circumstances. *Emotion, Space and Society, 9*, 59–71.

Duncombe, S. (2007). (From) Cultural resistance to community development. *Community Development Journal, 42*(4), 490–500.

Gordon, E. (2013). Under-served and un-deserving: Youth empowerment programs, poverty discourses and subject formation. *Geoforum, 50*, 107–116.

Hampshire, K., & Matthijsse, M. (2010). Can arts projects improve young people's wellbeing? A social capital approach. *Social Science & Medicine (1982), 71*(4), 708–716.

Ngo, B., Lewis, C., & Maloney Leaf, B. (2017). Fostering sociopolitical consciousness with minoritized youth: Insights from community-based arts programs. *Review of Research in Education, 41*(1), 358–380.

OUP. (2016–2020). *Outer urban projects strategic plan 2016–2020*. Melbourne.

OUP. (2022a). *Outer urban projects website*. Accessed 24 January 2022, https://www.outerurbanprojects.org

OUP. (2022b). *Outer urban projects Twitter*. Accessed 21 January 2022, https://twitter.com/outerurban

OUP. (2022c). *Outer urban projects website: Hume Studios*. Accessed 24 January 2022, https://www.outerurbanprojects.org/works/hume-studios/

OUP. (2022d). *Outer urban projects Vimeo: Trailer | Hume Studios*. Accessed 24 January 2022, https://vimeo.com/389600105

Parliament of Victoria. (2013, June). *Inquiry on growing the suburbs: Infrastructure and business development in outer suburban Melbourne*. Melbourne. Accessed 6 January 2022, https://www.parliament.vic.gov.au/images/stories/committees/osisdv/Growing_the_Suburbs/Growing_Suburbs_report.pdf

Roestone Collective. (2014). Safe space: Towards a reconceptualization. *Antipode, 46*, 1346–1365.

Throsby, D., & Petetskaya, K. (2017). *Making art work: An economic study of professional artists in Australia*. Australia Council for the Arts, Strawberry Hills, NSW.

Warr, D. (2006). Gender, class, and the art and craft of social capital. *Sociological Quarterly, 47*(3), 497–520.

Watts, R. (2013, October 9). Two-speed cities: Can art bridge the urban divide? *Artshub*. Accessed 6 January 2022, https://www.artshub.com.au/news/features/two-speed-cities-can-art-bridge-the-urban-divide-196923-2311125/

Wright, R., John, L., Alaggia, R., & Sheel, J. (2006). Community-based arts program for youth in low-income communities: A multi-method evaluation. *Child & Adolescent Social Work Journal, 23*(5), 635–652.

8

Conclusion

Abstract In this chapter we reflect on key questions and issues examined in the book. We explore the local and global contexts through which art-based social enterprises (ASEs) operate and within which they attempt—often successfully—to improve access to education and work for emerging creatives. We also attend to the findings generated through engaging with the lived experiences of the staff and young creatives involved in our ASE case studies, in order to understand both the challenges and impacts of the ASE model on young people's education, training, and employment pathways. This concluding chapter therefore brings together and conceptually synthesises the key themes of this book: aspiration, hope, complexity, ambivalence, resistance and contestation. In doing so, we contribute to debates about the limits, possibilities and challenges that attach to, and emerge from, an ASE model and we highlight the ways in which these models can contribute to young people's well-being, engagement, education and training, and work pathways. More broadly, we examine the possibilities of art as a means of social and cultural engagement. In the context of the precarious future of the creative industries we emphasise, in this concluding chapter, the ways in which young artists are building alternative economic and cultural models that support both individual pathways and collective change.

Keywords Art · Social enterprise · Education · Employment · Cultural resistance · Entrepreneurial · Creative industries · Young creatives · Wellbeing · Engagement · Youth transitions · Pathways

In this book, we have examined the local and global contexts through which ASEs operate and within which they attempt—often successfully—to improve access to education and work for emerging creatives. We have also attended to the complex and nuanced lived experiences of the staff and young creatives involved in ASEs, in order to understand both the challenges and impacts of the ASE model on young people's education, training and employment pathways. Alongside undertaking extensive qualitative research involving interviews and observation, we have purposefully collaborated with emerging creatives across our three case studies in workshops and exhibitions—and, through this, have expanded our analysis to consider the mechanics of creative processes, and the importance of material and artistic practices in engaging young people.

This concluding chapter brings together and conceptually synthesises the key themes of this book: aspiration, hope, complexity, ambivalence, resistance and contestation. In doing so, we contribute to debates about the limits, possibilities and challenges that attach to, and emerge from, an ASE model and we highlight the ways in which these models can contribute to young people's wellbeing, engagement, education and training, and work pathways. More broadly, we examine the possibilities of art as a means of social and cultural engagement. In the context of the precarious future of the creative industries, we emphasise, in these concluding comments, the ways in which young artists are building alternative economic and cultural models that support both individual pathways and collective change.

8 Conclusion

Creativity in a Time of Crisis

Young creatives require a significant reserve of resilience to navigate a path in the contemporary creative industries—which, as we have discussed, are marked by patterns of short-term work, competition, uncertainty and fluctuating markets. This precarity has been heightened by multiple crises, especially the global financial crisis of 2009, the COVID-19 pandemic and the ever more acute climate crisis. Each of these has signalled massive social and economic ramifications globally, all which have impacted on the arts, particularly evident in declining government funding for, and private investment in, cultural activities. For young creatives already impacted by forces of marginalisation and now contending with the disruptions of several years of lockdowns, travel restrictions and climate-based emergencies, simply engaging with and accessing education and work can be a formidable challenge, let alone forging a sustainable pathway into the creative industries. As we have argued in this book, ASEs are playing a unique role in supporting emerging artists to develop skills and confidence, to aspire to, hope for and imagine a future in the creative industries, and, in many cases, to develop practical pathways into further education and work in order to enable this. Importantly, beyond a deficit-lens of hardship and struggle, ASEs can help reorient young people impacted by marginalisation towards a critical awareness of their social and economic position and promote grounded aspiration for what Angela McRobbie points to as careers that are 'meaningful and rewarding' (2016, p. 118).

As we have documented and explored through a case study approach, the creative arts can offer a highly engaging and accessible entry point to education and work—we have seen this appeal in the realm of digital media which builds on the ubiquitous digital literacy of younger generations; in the material practices of textiles which transcend language and cultural barriers; and in the expressive qualities of performing arts media which enable young people to share their experiences in relation to their peers and community. The ASE model harnesses this potential for engagement through the arts broadly defined, and brings that creative realm into dialogue with education, training and potential employment. While ASEs are often under-resourced and must, like other enterprises, compete in markets in order to generate income, their emphasis on process as much, if not more so than, profit, is a model that can support the engagement of a range of young people experiencing barriers to education and employment.

As we have demonstrated throughout this book, the complexity and challenges of balancing social, economic and artistic goals are significant for ASEs and mirror the simultaneous challenges that young people face in navigating future careers in the precarious creative industries. In particular for ASEs, the SE sector, government, philanthropy and industry tend to emphasise hard measures of success—for example, profit margins, revenue, quantitative measures of employment and the ability to achieve 'scale'. Our analysis of ASEs has demonstrated that their contributions are much broader than this—and that by attending to the qualitative, human and lived experience of those involved in ASEs, we can gain a much deeper understanding of what social impact and social change actually look like in relation to the ASE model. In particular, we have observed the impacts of the ASE model in providing education and training that is relevant for the twenty-first century in terms of traversing the hard and soft skills necessary for workplaces of the future. However, it is important to note that the impact of ASEs, which work in specific art forms and in specific social contexts, cannot easily be generalised. It is for this reason that we have, in this book, surveyed a broader range of ASEs across Australia, considered international trends in the sectors of youth development and the arts, and then focused more specifically on three case studies—Youthworx, The Social Studio (TSS) and Outer Urban Projects (OUP)—to forge an analysis with scope and depth.

To reiterate, ASEs operate with vastly different art forms and they work with different communities. Understanding the varying material and cultural practices generated by working with different art media, and the diverse discourses of creativity arising from working with particular communities of young people, is crucial in considering the potential for ASEs to support pathways into work and study. Each of the conceptually contextualising chapters in this book demonstrates this. In Chapter 2, we explored the ways in which digital media engagement is being utilised, in a range of cultural contexts in Australia and elsewhere, to re-engage young people in education. Digital media taps into popular youth cultures including film and TV, music, gaming, social media and internet connectivity and develops a range of both hard skills, from competencies in media production and design, and soft skills, including storytelling, communication, collaboration and problem-solving. In Chapter 4, we looked at how the material practices of fashion and textiles are being harnessed, once again in specific cultural settings, to engage communities impacted by the forces of migration and displacement. Fashion and textile production can build on existing cultural strengths and bring traditional aesthetics into dialogue with contemporary cosmopolitan and urban cultures. Moreover, these material practices can support the development of income streams and activate learning and work opportunities by uniquely overcoming language and communication barriers. In Chapter 6, we looked at how gentrification is changing the shape of cities and forcing more and more populations of people into the outer fringe, with flow-on effects of disconnection from infrastructure, mainstream culture and employment opportunities. In the context of this, we looked at how performing arts practices in particular are being used to engage young people impacted by these spatialised forms of marginalisation and at how divisions between the cultures of the urban centre and suburban fringe are being challenged through creating bridging networks into the creative industries.

These themes were grounded in each of the focused chapters on our Melbourne-based case studies. As we discussed in Chapter 3, Youthworx has a strong track record in not only engaging young people in learning, but supporting their wellbeing and developing pathways—particularly for those who have disengaged from mainstream schooling—into further training and paid employment. Media training, in particular, was shown to support young people to develop not only confidence and skills, but to support improved mental health and wellbeing. As a well-established ASE, Youthworx is faced with the challenge of fitting creative media development into a formal vocational training model, while also having to deal with a significant disjunct between a focus on skill development and confidence building for their students and the highly competitive employment realities of the fast-paced environment of the mainstream media industry.

In Chapter 5, we turned our focus to the ways in which The Social Studio provides formal training and employment pathways for young creatives from refugee and migrant backgrounds through engagement with fashion and textiles. While the organisation promotes sustainability and social impact, they operate in an industry notorious for exploitation and environmental waste, and therefore have to balance aspirations for growth with the realities of operating counter to industry norms. Likewise, TSS students and emerging designers counterbalance their own creative and professional aspirations with realistic expectations—what we have described as their 'pragmatic ambitions'. Nevertheless, the young creatives at TSS are forging meaningful and rewarding pathways into both further education and work, in a space that privileges their artistic and cultural strengths.

Finally, our discussion of Outer Urban Projects in Chapter 7 turned to how OUP supports and activates the creative talents of young people living in the outer northern suburbs of Melbourne, and does so across a range of performing arts platforms from rap and spoken work, to music, dance and song. By providing a vehicle for creative expression and, in particular, the activation of voice, we examined how OUP enables the development of counter-cultural, democratising practices for their emerging artists. We further explored how OUP navigates a central tension between promoting the 'success stories' of those engaged with OUP programs and attending also to the socio-economic realities of their young artists' lives. OUP artists are similarly navigating a path that includes both personal aspirations for success (and in some cases fame) with an equal desire to give back and contribute to their own communities.

As the case study chapters have demonstrated, Youthworx, The Social Studio and Outer Urban Projects occupy quite different areas in the creative industries, while they work also with different populations of young people that, in turn, gives rise to different operational and pedagogical challenges. Yet we have also found that all three organisations are connected by several common denominators. All three tend towards an implicit—and sometimes explicit—critique of mainstream business approaches and discourses, and they hold varying aspirations to contest and transform the commercial frameworks of the creative industries in which they operate (McRobbie, 2016). They are thus connected by a focus on creating spaces of collectivity and belonging, values which are privileged over 'hard' measures of success and profit—and yet which, we argue, are the essential precursors to supporting young people into further work and study. Each of these three social enterprises also, of course, deploys creativity as a means to connect and engage with young people, and to facilitate the development of both technical and creative skills that open up pathways into further education and work. Further, all three social enterprises share experiences of organisational struggle in precarious markets and face an increasingly pressurised nonprofit sector. This clear commonality, especially in relation to contesting and reframing dominant commercial logics, speaks to the point first raised in Chapter 1; ASEs, and certainly the case study organisations examined here, align with broader movements advocating and modelling alternative forms of market engagement and new performances of economy. This, as we have discussed at numerous points throughout the book, leaves our case study organisations—and those who work within them—in a highly ambiguous relationship to the conventional commercial goals of enterprise and engenders, by necessity as much as by design, an ethos of contesting the market.

At the level of day-to-day practices, our three case study organisations also share some important features, especially in terms of what might be called mechanisms of engagement. Firstly, we found that all three organisations provided opportunities for young creatives to access bridging networks—networks of professional and emerging artists, cultural organisations, businesses, education providers and community partners—that activated possible pathways into both education (e.g. vocational training qualifications at Youthworx and The Social Studio that facilitate pathways into higher education) and paid work in the creative industries (e.g. opportunities to show work at major cultural institutions like the Arts Centre Melbourne for artists at Outer Urban Projects). Secondly, we found that each of the case study organisations provided an important space of belonging for young artists to come to, and importantly, to return to. This pointed to the strong sense of engagement that young artists developed by being involved in creative training—an engagement that was much more likely to be longer term rather than short term, and that was indelibly linked to a sense of social connection and wellbeing. Developing this sense of confidence and wellbeing, in turn, was linked to young peoples' pursuit of further employment and education pathways.

Thirdly, we found that having a context for *learning to learn* is an essential skill for young people experiencing disengagement from education (Deakin et al., 2014). A common feature of the education and training approaches across the three ASEs was the opportunity to collaborate or work in group settings, which we found promoted both a sense of social inclusion (articulated above) and also opening up the possibility of shared understandings of identity, place and culture. Through creativity and artistic expression, for example, many young people across the three ASEs were able to articulate or creatively express their understanding of the world, and reflect on social and political challenges pertinent to their lives, with the potential to develop new subjectivities. In particular, we noted a shared interest across the ASEs in moving away from deficit constructions of young peoples' identities and towards formations of identity that emphasise agency, artistic talent and sociopolitical consciousness.

One further key point of commonality across the three case study organisations moves us towards some of the broader implications of this study. In order for ASEs to provide mechanisms and opportunities for young peoples' engagement, it is imperative that the organisations themselves are aware of, and have strategies to address, the specific structural inequalities—and forces of marginalisation—that are relevant to their differing communities (Dreher, 2012; Tuck, 2009). In this context, we have identified a number of strategies that address structural barriers at Youthworx, TSS and OUP that are clearly relevant more widely for ASEs and arts organisations wishing to engage diverse cohorts of young people. Simple strategies, such as providing transport and purchasing equipment, enabled greater participation for young people. Engaging family members to understand and appreciate the benefits of arts engagement was another key strategy we identified. Offering incentives to participate, for example opportunities to get paid work or 'gigs', was also key for young artists experiencing financial hardship across all three case studies.

Importantly, recognising and working with existing cultural capital (e.g. musical talents already developed in a family or community context;

or cultural fashion influences) rather than simply introducing new skills and creative forms that are not relevant to young people from more diverse cultural and social backgrounds was a central strategy of respectful engagement observed across the three case studies—a finding confirmed in similar research on youth community arts engagement (Hampshire & Matthijsse, 2010). Further, recognising structural inequalities may also mean accepting, as Elyse Gordon argues, that many young people may simply fail, or often disengage (2013). As we have documented, this logic was built into the accredited and professional training models across the three case studies. Rather than selecting the most motivated and aspirational young creatives for engagement, therefore, ASEs might consider building opportunities for young people most at risk of failing.

At a broader level also, this study suggests that by modelling alternative approaches to education and employment for young artists, ASEs have the potential to demonstrate to industry and educational providers the possibility and benefits of offering forms of engagement and employment that are, above all, inclusive. The transformative potential of these inclusive models of education and employment was most evident in our study when we noted examples of young artists replicating what they had learnt through ASE involvement within their own community contexts. For example, when graduates of TSS started their own social enterprises; when students at Youthworx wanted to share their skills with peers and other young creatives; and when artists at OUP talked about wanting to start up their own community dance or music studios to support young people. Here, we found one of the most obvious, and yet least expected outcomes of the ASE model in our study: by enacting alternative models of creative arts entrepreneurship that privilege community, creative expression and collective ways of making over the pursuit of profits or individual gain, ASEs are developing pathways for young artists towards alternative and more critical forms of cultural production. In turn, these young artists may aspire to contest and change the very fabric of the creative industries.

Through our analysis, it has become abundantly clear that ASEs are organisations dealing in and juggling with seemingly contradictory outcomes. On the one hand, they aim to educate and train creative workers and entrepreneurs who must struggle as often self-employed individuals in a precarious, unequal and underpaid gig economy. On the other hand, ASEs generate supportive spaces that encourage hopeful, resilient communities of young artists that have the potential to reshape unequal cultural structures, change perceptions of marginality and produce new, sustainable art worlds. These mixed outcomes are not a reflection on ASEs themselves, but on the world in which they operate: a world in which the pursuit of social goals is weighted against economic and social structures that privilege the pursuit of profit. This seeming contradiction at the heart of ASE activity, therefore, actually reveals the complexity of privileging forms of social collectivity that are at odds with the imperatives of mainstream market forces. That is, contradiction and the sense of ambivalent positionality it gives rise to may be a necessary condition of trying to contest dominant logics and create change from 'within'. As we discussed in Chapter 1, forms of social enterprise in the arts are increasingly understood as aligning with a politics of resistance that is understood to emerge from within capitalist systems while focusing, at the same time, on improving outcomes for artists and promoting artistic agency (Lee Wong, 2019, McRobbie, 2011).

In line with these patterns of resistance and contestation, a final key finding of this book is that the majority of ASEs we have surveyed appear to be challenging dominant trends, not simply within mainstream commerce, but within the SE sector itself. As we have noted, social enterprise is a growing form of commerce that is increasingly of interest to government, philanthropy and the private sector for promising to deliver social outcomes while simultaneously promoting business models that can scale, grow and achieve financial sustainability. The SE sector also values hard measures of social impact, including, for example, quantitative employment outcomes and financial measures of 'return on investment' (Denny & Seddon, 2013). In the context of these trends, we have observed that ASEs are, in large part, more focused on the deep, human and, at times, gritty work of addressing structural inequalities. Moreover, ASEs appear to place greater emphasis on working against mainstream market logics and on working with smaller groups of people over longer periods of time. As a result, they rarely achieve SE industry expectations in terms of profit-generation, scale and quantitative outcomes.

Above all, we have found that ASEs are focused on creating spaces for emerging artists to come to and return to, spaces where people can both belong and create. In these spaces, young creatives are developing confidence and hope, exploring individual and collective identities, finding wellbeing, and developing aspirations for the future. The ASE model, therefore, has significant potential not only to support young people impacted by forces of marginalisation (economic, social, neoliberal, neocolonial), but to also benefit young people more broadly, a population that is increasingly bearing the brunt of the numerous local and global crises that are coming to define work and education in the twenty-first century.

References

Deakin, C. R., Stringher, C., & Ren, K. (Eds.). (2014). *Learning to learn: International perspectives from theory and practice*. Taylor & Francis Group.

Denny, S., & Seddon, F. (Eds). (2013). *Social enterprise: Accountability and evaluation around the world*. Taylor & Francis Group.

Dreher, T. (2012). 'A partial promise of voice: Digital storytelling and the limits of listening' [Paper in themed section: The media's role in social inclusion and exclusion]. *Media International Australia Incorporating Culture & Policy, 142*, 157–166.

Gordon, E. (2013). Under-served and un-deserving: Youth empowerment programs, poverty discourses and subject formation. *Geoforum, 50*, 107–116.

Hampshire, K., & Matthijsse, M. (2010). Can arts projects improve young people's wellbeing? A social capital approach. *Social Science & Medicine (1982), 71*(4), 708–716.

Lee Wong, A. (2019). Artists as enterprise: Incorporating as forms of organising agencies. *PARSE Journal, 9*(Spring).

McRobbie, A. (2011). Re-thinking creative economy as radical social enterprise. *Variant, 41*, 32–33.

McRobbie, A. (2016). *Be creative: Making a living in the new culture industries*. Polity Press.

Tuck, E. (2009). Suspending damage: A letter to communities. *Harvard Educational Review, 79*(3), 409–427; 539–540.

Index

A

Accredited/accreditation 33, 37, 60, 84, 99, 153
Ambivalent/ambivalence 13, 21, 84, 86, 95, 134, 146, 154
Art-based social enterprise/s (ASE/s) 2, 6, 10, 13, 17–21, 33, 37, 44, 67, 84, 108, 109, 118, 142, 143, 146–149, 153–155
Aspiration 20, 21, 51, 75, 143, 146, 147

B

Belonging 51, 62, 98, 112, 130, 151
Bonding networks 34, 130, 136
Bridging networks 21, 34, 35, 54, 116, 129–131, 136, 142, 149, 151

C

Case study/ies 5, 10, 12, 18–20, 37, 43, 49, 58, 72, 77, 84, 94, 95, 114, 118, 124, 135, 146–153
Collaboration 19, 22, 43, 58, 74, 115, 116, 126, 131, 149
Collectivity 151, 154
Commodification 36
Community xi, 2, 8, 13, 30, 31, 36, 45, 50, 58, 69, 70, 73, 85–90, 92, 94, 96, 98, 101, 104, 109, 110, 113, 118, 122, 125–131, 138, 140–143, 147, 151–153
Community arts xii, 12, 13, 113, 115, 124, 129, 153
Complexity 10, 21, 43, 72, 84, 86, 99, 112, 146, 148, 154
Confidence 21, 29, 32–34, 43, 50, 51, 55, 58, 74, 75, 85–88, 90,

91, 97, 114, 137, 147, 149, 152, 155
Contestation 21, 146, 154
Covid-19 3, 11, 33, 43, 68, 147
Craftivism 69, 70
Creative digital media 13, 20, 28–31, 34, 36, 37
Creative industries 2, 3, 5–7, 10, 13, 14, 20, 21, 32, 37, 43, 47, 49, 50, 61, 67, 68, 94, 95, 97, 108, 116–118, 135, 136, 143, 146–151, 153
Creative practices 10, 13, 61, 66, 69, 74, 91, 102, 108, 111, 112, 134
Crisis/crises xii, 3, 4, 8, 10, 30, 43, 68, 128, 147, 155
Cultural citizenship 13, 112, 114, 118, 138
Cultural resistance 115, 137

D

Digital media 7, 29–33, 35–37, 42, 45, 52, 53, 61, 147, 148
Displacement 12, 20, 66, 71, 72, 84, 86, 101, 102, 104, 108, 109, 149
Dreher, Tania 36, 44, 59, 114

E

Education and training 2, 3, 8–10, 16, 20, 28, 33, 34, 146, 148, 152
Employment 2–4, 6, 9–11, 15, 20–22, 28–35, 37, 42–51, 62, 66, 67, 72, 76, 77, 84, 103, 104, 116, 122, 147–149, 152–154
Employment pathways 2, 7, 11, 32, 33, 45, 61, 126, 146, 150
Engagement xii, 6–8, 12, 13, 15, 20, 21, 31, 32, 34, 35, 37, 43, 46, 50, 52, 53, 61, 62, 87, 94, 97, 108, 111, 115, 116, 122, 128, 135, 139, 146–148, 150–153
Entrepreneurial 7, 8, 13, 15, 17, 21, 29, 50, 71, 76, 116, 118, 131, 132

F

Fashion 7, 13, 14, 19, 20, 66–68, 71–73, 76, 77, 82–88, 91, 93–96, 98, 99, 103, 104, 149, 150, 153
Flexibility 7–9, 54, 73, 75, 89, 100, 101
Forces of marginalisation 4, 5, 11, 18, 22, 49, 53, 61, 62, 73, 108, 117, 147, 152, 155
Fourth industrial revolution 2, 7

G

Gentrification 108–110, 126, 149
Gerrard, Jessica 5, 36
Gigs/gigging 7, 50, 123, 128, 132, 154
Gordon, Elyse 12, 100, 114, 128, 153

H

Higher education 94, 97, 151
Homeless/ness 45, 46, 60

I

Inequality 36, 37, 111, 116, 125, 137, 142
Interest-driven learning 53

L

Learn to learn/learning to learn 33, 74, 97

M

Mainstream 3, 9, 13, 17, 21, 33, 34, 42, 44, 49, 53, 54, 61, 62, 66, 75, 90, 96, 99, 103, 104, 116, 124, 125, 136, 138, 141, 142, 149, 150, 154
Marginalisation 4, 5, 11, 12, 17, 20, 31, 36, 45, 48, 58, 60, 68, 71, 75, 108, 109, 125, 126, 138–140, 147, 149
Markets 7, 8, 15–17, 32, 68, 70, 86, 109, 134, 141, 147, 148
Material practice 11, 20, 66, 147, 149
McRobbie, Angela 6, 7, 15–17, 67, 73, 76, 77, 86, 88, 147, 151, 154
Migration 12, 20, 66, 71, 72, 84–86, 88, 101, 102, 104, 149

N

Neighbourhood 34, 109–112, 116, 130
Neoliberalism 8, 11, 15, 16
Nonprofit 151

O

OECD 2–4, 11, 28, 35, 85
Outcomes 10, 18, 21, 22, 31, 35, 37, 46, 48, 50, 51, 58, 61, 72, 74–76, 85, 87, 90, 98, 102, 103, 108, 116, 143, 153–155
Outer Urban Projects (OUP) 5, 7, 10, 12, 18–21, 43, 56, 118, 122–143, 148, 150–153

P

Pandemic xii, 3, 43, 68, 147
Performing arts 7, 13, 20, 21, 43, 108, 112–114, 118, 123, 125, 127, 132, 135, 136, 140, 147, 150
Post-capitalism 16
Postcode 108, 111, 130
Pragmatic ambition/s 77, 84, 150
Precarity 2, 3, 20, 118, 135, 142, 147
Precursors 21, 29, 33, 50, 103, 151
Professional 21, 34, 43, 46, 54–56, 58, 59, 62, 86, 94, 97, 101, 116, 117, 123, 124, 126, 127, 129, 130, 132–134, 140, 142, 150, 151, 153
Profit 10, 16, 29, 32, 76, 88, 148, 151, 153–155
Public/s xi, 7, 10, 17, 19, 53, 58, 59, 69, 70, 76, 87, 100, 111, 116, 118, 131, 140

R

Resistance 21, 113, 146, 154

S

Scale 9, 12, 68, 73, 76, 95, 104, 125, 126, 148, 154, 155
Social capital 34, 54, 67, 72, 73, 112, 116, 117, 130, 136, 142
Social enterprise xi, 2, 4–6, 8–14, 16, 22, 32, 35, 37, 42, 45, 49, 50, 60, 66, 67, 71, 72, 75–77, 84, 85, 87, 88, 99, 123, 127, 131, 141, 151, 153, 154
Social impact 14, 76, 84, 103, 128, 148, 150, 154
Socially engaged art xi
Social Studio. *See* The Social Studio (TSS)
Social turn 2
Socio-economic disadvantage 4, 114
Sociopolitical consciousness 21, 112, 137, 152
Spatialised disadvantage 149
Stigma 11, 111, 112
Structural change 45, 61, 114, 115, 118, 124, 140, 143
Studio 46, 47, 56, 88, 94, 103, 133–135
Systemic 21, 62, 87, 100

T

Teaching 7, 43, 56, 85, 89–91, 95, 101, 128, 132–135, 140
Textile/s 7, 13, 20, 45, 66, 69–71, 74, 84–86, 89, 91–94, 102, 103, 147, 149, 150
The Social Studio (TSS) 7, 10, 12, 14, 18–20, 72, 77, 82, 84–104, 148, 150–153
Transitions 20, 21, 28, 35, 50, 51, 60, 61, 86, 141, 142
Tuck, Eve 4, 18
Twenty-first-century skills 7, 29, 50, 97

U

UNESCO 3, 6, 7, 30, 33, 66, 68, 69, 86
Urban fringe 108, 109, 111–113, 115–118, 124, 142

V

Vocational 15, 33, 37, 60, 61, 75, 76, 84, 92, 93, 149, 151
Voice 4, 18–20, 31, 36, 44, 55, 59, 62, 112, 113, 123, 126, 137, 138, 142, 150

W

Wellbeing xii, 7, 21, 31, 35, 36, 43, 46, 50, 51, 59, 61, 72, 103, 108, 137, 149, 152, 155

Y

Young creatives 15, 16, 31, 54, 66, 67, 75, 77, 94–96, 103, 117, 127, 142, 143, 146, 147, 150, 151, 153, 155
Youthworx 4, 5, 7, 10, 12, 18–20, 37, 42–62, 97, 148–153

Ingram Content Group UK Ltd.
Milton Keynes UK
UKHW020145050723
424579UK00004B/275